AU SM PRAISE

Leading a team isn't just about the moments in the spotlight—it's about the commitment, resilience, and heart you bring to every challenge, on and off the ice. In Be Au Sm, Josh Peach delivers a powerful reminder that living your legacy starts with how you show up every day. His message of Gratitude, Resilience, Action, Consistency, and Empowerment is exactly what we need to inspire the next generation to lead with purpose and heart.

— **Mike Eruzione, Captain, 1980 U.S. Olympic Gold Medal Hockey Team**

Just as I learned that it's not about the coffee but about the people, Josh Peach shows us that it's not about theories but about purposeful action. His G.R.A.C.E. framework aligns beautifully with the principles of servant leadership, showing us how to lead with authenticity, uplift those around us, and create a lasting impact. This book is a must-read for anyone looking to serve, inspire, and leave the world better than they found it.

— **Howard Behar, retired President of Starbucks Coffee Company International and author of *It's Not About the Coffee***

Josh Peach's *Be Au Sm* is a masterclass in living with presence and purpose. His words will empower you to strive for greatness while staying grounded in gratitude.

— **Fred Makonnen, Head of Sales & Distribution, Group Retirement, Equitable**

AU SM PRAISE

Some books entertain... some books educate... and then there are books like *Be Au Sm*...books that inspire action and challenge you to level up in how you show up for yourself and others. Joshua Peach delivers an energizing, no-excuses guide to leading with G.R.A.C.E., and he does it through real, relatable stories that stick with you long after you put the book down. This isn't theory... it's lived experience, told in a way that makes you laugh, reflect, and, most importantly, act. If you're looking for a book that's part motivational kick-in-the-ass, part leadership playbook, and 100% authentic, this is it.

— **Jon Macaskill, Ret. Navy SEAL Commander, mindfulness teacher, leadership coach, and resilience expert**

True resilience isn't about surviving a single life-altering moment—it's about the choices we make every day. In *Be Au Sm*, Josh Peach gives us the framework to build a life of purpose, impact, and unwavering strength. His words challenge us to stop waiting for the perfect moment and start living our legacy now.

—**Aron Ralston, author, speaker, and inspiration for *127 Hours*.**

Josh Peach is the real deal. His stories are authentic, deeply personal, and universally relatable. In *Be Au Sm*, he reminds us that gratitude, resilience, and action are essential elements to living a purposeful life. Josh captures what it means to be truly awesome: living with passion, purpose, and a daily commitment to making a difference.

—-**James M. Rowan, CAE, SFO, CEO, ASBO International**

AU SM PRAISE

Be Au Sm is more than a book—it's a blueprint for showing up with purpose, resilience, and an unwavering commitment to performance excellence. As a career US Army officer, Special Operations Veteran, and a Mental Performance and Leadership Coach in pro football, I know firsthand that success isn't just about talent; it's about mindset, consistency, and developing the skills to lead with authenticity. Josh Peach masterfully distills the essence of leadership, gratitude, and action into a powerful framework (GRACE) that resonates across any profession, from the battlefield to the boardroom, from the locker room to everyday life. This book is a must-read for anyone looking to elevate their leadership and leave a lasting impact.

—US Army Lt Col (Ret.) Andy Riise Mental Performance and Leadership Coach for the Chicago Bears

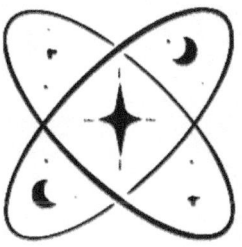

The Essential Elements to Living Your Legacy with G.R.A.C.E.

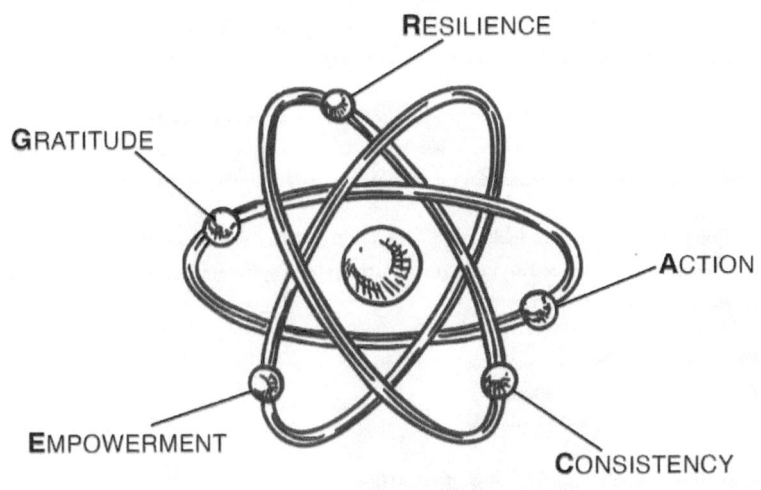

JOSHUA PEACH
MARK J RESNICK

Published by Bellarmine Publishing LLC

Bellarmine Publishing books, including *Be Au Sm*, are available at special discounts for bulk purchases, sales promotions, or corporate use. Custom cover wraps are also available upon request. Contact: mark@markjresnick.com.

ISBN: 979-8-9857494-8-9 Paperback
ISBN: 979-8-9857494-9-6 eBook
ISBN: 979-8-9923591-0-7 Hardcover

Library of Congress Control Number:2025903894

Bellarmine
PUBLISHING, LLC

To Amy, Danny, and Chance,
for letting me be the most okay person you know

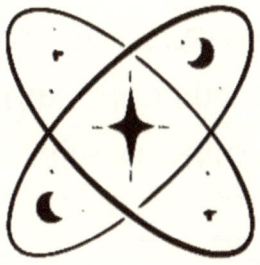

To Coleen, Campbell, Erin, and Sean,
for letting me be me

CONTENTS

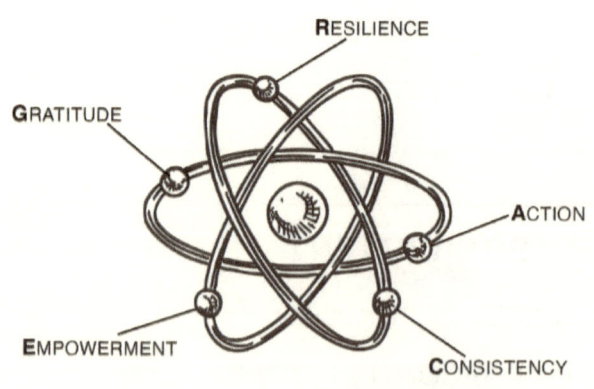

Live Your Legacy

FOREWORD

BY SANTA CLAUS

The origins of Santa Claus can be traced back to St. Nicholas, a 4th-century Greek bishop known for his generosity, kindness, and legendary miracles. My name, Santa Claus, is derived from the Dutch expression for St. Nicholas: Sinterklaas. His legacy of selflessness and giving has endured for over 1,700 years, evolving into the Santa we know today—the one who brings joy to children around the world.

But the truth is: Santa was never about gifts under the tree. Santa has always been about something much greater—spreading hope, kindness, and love.

There are moments in life when you meet someone and instantly recognize that they are meant to be part of your journey. That's how I felt when I first met Josh Peach. He was just a guy with a podcast, calling me from across the country, asking me to share my story. But what struck me about Josh wasn't just his persistence—it was his heart.

Josh doesn't just talk about living your legacy—he embodies it. Through *Be Au Sm*, he delivers a message that the world needs now more than ever: that a life of meaning isn't something we leave behind, but rather something we live every day.

I legally changed my name to Santa Claus not as a gimmick, but as a commitment to service—to dedicate my life to protecting children, fighting for those in need, and reminding the world that love is the greatest gift we can give.

That's why, when the time came for me to pass on my Santa suit, I knew exactly who should have it. I didn't give it to Josh because he's famous or successful—I gave it to him because he understands what Santa has always stood for. He understands that small acts of kindness can change lives and that living with G.R.A.C.E.—Gratitude, Resilience, Action, Consistency, and Empowerment—is how we create a lasting legacy.

Be Au Sm is more than just a guide—it's an invitation. Josh challenges each of us to live boldly, to lead with heart, and to embrace the elements of G.R.A.C.E. in ways that truly impact the world around us. Most importantly, he reminds us that our greatest legacy isn't measured in titles, possessions, or achievements—it's measured in love.

Be Au Sm isn't just about self-improvement. It's about choosing to be a light in the world, even when it feels dark.

Be Au Sm is about love.

So, as you read these pages, ask yourself this: *What will my legacy be?* Because you don't need a red suit or a sleigh to be Santa Claus. You just need a heart willing to give, to help others, and to spread the kind of joy and kindness that lasts far beyond a single season.

Wishing you a lifetime filled with happiness, peace, good health, prosperity, and, most of all, love—because love is, and always will be, the greatest gift of all.

Santa Claus
North Pole, Alaska
Mayor Pro Tem / Councilman, City of North Pole / Child Advocate

INTRODUCTION

BY JOSHUA PEACH

What comes to mind when you think about the word legacy?

For many, it's something you leave behind—a mark on the world, something people remember you by. But living your legacy isn't about waiting until the end to see what you've built. It's about the choices you make every day, in real time. It's about being present, making an impact, and ensuring that when you look back, you don't feel weighed down by regrets, wishing you had done more, been more, or spent more time with the people who mattered most.

That all sounds great, right? But let's be honest—living your legacy isn't always easy. It's hard to feel purposeful when you're exhausted, overwhelmed, or unsure of your direction. I know this because I've met countless people who've shared their struggles with me after my talks. People who felt stuck in jobs that drained them, lost in goals that no longer inspired them, or buried under the weight of responsibilities that made them question their own worth.

I understand that feeling because I've been there—I was one of those people.

Life is a gift, but let's not pretend it's always easy. We experience lousy luck, toxic relationships, poor health, aging parents, bad timing, and missed opportunities. These things can pull us under, making it hard to recognize the impact we are making, let alone believe we're capable of something greater. And sometimes, those struggles run deep.

For me, it started in childhood, a time filled with uncertainty and unanswered questions. I spent three years apart from my mother while she worked to build a future for us. It was a lonely time, and it left a mark.

I took five years to graduate high school and never finished college, and for a long time, I believed that meant I was a failure. That belief shaped the way I saw myself. It led me to make reckless choices, stuck in a cycle of doubt and frustration, constantly wondering *Why can't I just catch a break?*

As a kid, I thought I knew what legacy meant because I had grown up watching my biological father, who was rich and successful. I thought his fame and wealth were what legacy was all about. But as I got older, I realized his legacy wasn't something I wanted any part of. It was empty, based on surface-level success rather than real impact or relationships. My biological father's legacy was a phony.

Before I discovered how I wanted to live my legacy, I chased transactional relationships—ones that were all about getting something in return. But those relationships don't last. They're not genuine, there's no loyalty, and for a long time, I was okay with that because I thought that's how you "got ahead." But there's no place in my life anymore for people who are only out to serve themselves.

Now, I'm in a much better place. I live my legacy as best I can and share it with anyone willing to listen. I've learned a lot—through tears, heartbreak, and flat-out bad judgment. I didn't respect myself for a long time, and I definitely didn't see my potential. I was consumed with self-pity, and my constant companions were anger, sadness, regret, and resentment.

But despite all the baggage we might carry, despite the challenges we might face, the choice to live our legacy is ours. We can spend our lives blaming the past or ourselves, or we can choose to move forward, one step at a time.

Being Au Sm—truly awesome—takes work, just like anything else. Don't worry about being perfect; simply aim to make good choices more often than bad ones. Live in a way that honors who you are and what you can offer the world.

So, how do you live your legacy?

It starts with a shift in perspective, which is where G.R.A.C.E. comes in. The five elements—Gratitude, Resilience, Action, Consistency, and Empowerment—are the framework for living your legacy. They're not skills you're born with or privileges reserved for a few. They're principles that, when practiced, help you create a lasting impact—not just for yourself, but for others.

For me, it took years to realize that success didn't involve chasing the next deal, the next job, or the next superficial connection. I didn't need to prove myself to people who didn't matter. Instead, I could build a life rooted in values that actually meant something.

Each element of G.R.A.C.E. played a role in that transformation. Gratitude helped me appreciate what I had instead of dwelling on what I'd lost. Resilience kept me going when I felt like giving up. Action taught me that hoping for change wasn't enough—I had to take responsibility for making it happen. Consistency reminded me that showing up, even on the hard days, was what truly mattered. And Empowerment? That one took the longest to understand—but once I did, I realized that lifting others was the key to lifting myself, too.

That doesn't mean living with purpose and passion is easy. And it won't always come naturally. There are still days—plenty of them, in fact—when I don't feel Au Sm, but because I've surrounded myself with the right people and the right attitude, I wake up every day determined to try.

That's the key.

We won't be Au Sm all the time. We'll stumble, we'll fall, and we'll face setbacks. But if we keep our eyes on the elements that build us up rather than tear us down, we move in the right direction—forward.

Here's my message to you: Start living your legacy with G.R.A.C.E. today.

Don't wait for tomorrow or when you're in a good mood. Start right now. I'll do whatever I can to help you move forward and master these elements. If you reach out to me, I'll respond. But at the end of the day, being Au Sm is a choice. The power to live your legacy with G.R.A.C.E. is in your hands.

Thank you for being part of my Au Sm journey.

Josh Peach
508-238-5711

GRATITUDE

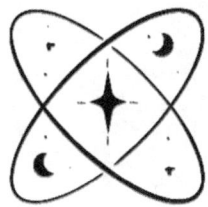

GRATITUDE HAS BEEN THE foundation of Be Au Sm from the beginning. It's so much more than saying "thank you."

Gratitude is our ability to shift perspectives—from what's missing to what's meaningful, from frustration to appreciation, and from obstacles to opportunities. It allows us to appreciate the people who shape our lives and to show up with an open heart, no matter the circumstances.

We can't just be thankful for the best days—we must find something to be thankful for on the toughest days. And gratitude isn't passive—it's a choice. Choose it daily, and it changes everything.

1

UNDER MY ROOF THIS WHOLE TIME

GRATITUDE

My oldest son, Danny, lost his father when he was 17 days old.

Because I'm not his biological father, we don't share the same last name. We differ in other ways, too. Danny is 6'6"—I barely top out at 6'. He loves everything and everyone—I don't. He's the most optimistic, happy-go-lucky, and patient person I know. Despite all our differences, Danny has shaped my life in ways I never imagined.

If Danny had not come into my life, I'm not sure I'd be here to write these words. Before him, I was at one of the lowest points in my life. I'd been through a string of bad relationships, each failure amplifying my self-doubt. My confidence was shattered. The economy wasn't helping either; it was the Great Recession, unemployment was through the roof, and the house I was renting and planning to purchase had lost a third of its value almost overnight. I felt like I was stuck in a cycle of disappointment and self-pity.

Professionally, I was also struggling. My sales weren't the issue. I was performing well despite the uncertain economic climate. But I was having difficulty getting booked to speak at industry tradeshows, where educational sessions (really thinly veiled sales pitches) were highly valued by my company. I hated the canned nature of those presentations, and to make matters worse, nobody wanted to give me a shot. Without a track record, I couldn't get booked. And without bookings, I couldn't build a track record. It was a frustrating cycle, and each rejection felt like another blow to my already fragile confidence.

Then Danny became part of my life, which equally enchanted and terrified me. Based on past relationships, especially the ones that didn't go so well, I was panicked that I wouldn't be a good father. I was so afraid to screw it up, insecure about my role in his life. On the other hand, Danny's presence gave me hope that maybe, just maybe, I could avoid the mistakes of my non-biological fathers.

Still, I doubted myself.

THE DEFINING MOMENT

But a pivotal moment came in October 2008. I was at the Sheraton in downtown Denver, sharing a drink with my friend John Musso. John was a mentor and a lifeline during those difficult years. Before heading to a top-tier event he'd invited me to crash, he handed me a copy of Randy Pausch's the *Last Lecture*. "Read this," he said, "and tell me what you think."

It took me a few months to finally read the book, but it was worth it. Pausch was essentially saying, "live your legacy" every day, and his words resonated. I was lucky to have someone like John in my life then, but his pulling me aside to share the book and listen to my problems wasn't the most memorable part of the night.

That came when Amy called. "Danny wants to talk to you," she said. I was excited but cautious. At eighteen months old, I wasn't expecting much.

He got on the phone. Nothing.

Then, the most incredible four-letter word I've ever heard came out of his mouth: "Papa."

One word. Four letters. And my world shifted.

In that moment, I stopped doubting my ability to be a parent. Danny's "Papa" erased years of insecurity and self-doubt. It didn't matter that we didn't share the same last name or DNA. What mattered was that Danny saw me as his Papa. And that was all I needed.

SURROUNDED BY G.R.A.C.E.

Over the years, my speaking career took off. I went from being the guy who couldn't get booked to delivering more than a thousand talks across North America—from Nova Scotia, Canada, to North Pole, Alaska, and everywhere in between. I've learned something from every presentation and every person I've met along the way. But the truth is, over the last seventeen years, I've learned more from Danny than just about anybody.

His sense of humor, patience, tolerance for other opinions, kindness, amazing heart, and intelligence have inspired and lifted me up more times than I can count. Danny is the model representative of someone who is living his life with G.R.A.C.E.

Gratitude isn't just about saying thank you. It's about recognizing the people who make your life worth living and showing them, through your actions, that you don't take them for granted. For me, Danny embodies that lesson.

Danny's influence on my life has never wavered. He continues to shape my values, personality, and confidence in ways I never imagined were possible.

And he's been living under my roof this whole time.

2

FIRST DATE, FIRST WAKE

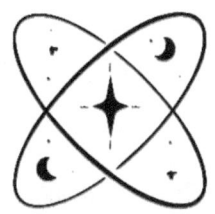

GRATITUDE

THE MOST UNUSUAL FIRST date of my life took me to a wake.

I was in high school, and I had asked a girl out for the following Friday's football game and a house party afterward. She said yes, and I was excited. But just a couple of days later, tragedy struck—one of her childhood friends died. The wake was scheduled for the same night as our first date.

This was the first death of a student our high school community had experienced in years, and it hit everyone hard. Many of my friends were planning to attend the wake to pay their respects. It didn't feel right to go to a party instead, so I offered to accompany my date to the wake, thinking it was the respectful thing to do.

Leading up to that Friday night, I asked a few people with "wake experience" what I should do—how to act, what to say, whether to pray, and how long to stay. I thought I was prepared.

We drove twenty minutes to the funeral home, making small talk on the way. There was an almost surreal sense to it all—who would have thought a first date could involve something so somber? We joked about how it would be one for the history books. But as we parked and walked to the funeral home, reality sank in. The line of people waiting to pay their respects was long, and the gravity of the situation began to weigh on me. I remember thinking, "What am I doing here? Why didn't I suggest going out another time?"

As we got closer to the casket, my nerves kicked in. My date noticed and whispered, "Don't worry, I'll go up with you so you're not alone." I felt a wave of relief, but in typical teenage fashion, I failed to express my gratitude. My ego was too focused on not appearing weak or out of place.

When we reached the casket, we knelt, made the sign of the cross, and sat in silence. My date was likely praying; my mind was racing with anxiety. I tried to focus on offering a prayer, but all I could think about was how out of my depth I felt.

UNINTENDED PAIN RESURFACES

Then, we moved on to the line of family members. I shook the father's hand and offered my condolences— "I'm sorry for your loss"—and did the same for the mother and other family members. But when I reached the girl's older sister, we'll call her Cindy, she was sitting in a chair, sobbing and clearly devastated. Cindy and I had gone to grade school together, but as the class sizes had expanded, we had lost touch. I recognized her and felt compelled to offer my condolences.

"Cindy, I'm sorry for your loss," I said.

What happened next was something I never could have anticipated. Cindy stopped sobbing and looked up at me. I thought she might thank me like the others had, but instead, she stood up. My date went to say something, but Cindy cut her off. Cindy looked me straight in the eye and said, "You are the last person in the world I would have expected to be here!"

I was paralyzed. Wait, I came here to pay respects, just like everyone else, I thought. But then, Cindy grabbed my hand and took me to her parents, interrupting the others who were offering their condolences.

"Mom, Dad, remember in grade school when I came home crying? This is the person who made me cry."

I was floored. Here I was, trying to offer support, and instead, I was the cause of old pain resurfacing. I stood there, facing Cindy's parents, who were already grieving the loss of their youngest child, now confronted with memories of the pain their oldest had suffered years ago—because of me. I fumbled for words, "I'm very sorry. I never meant to make anyone cry . . . we were just kids."

Cindy's parents were gracious, brushing it off with a simple, "Thank you for coming." But the damage was done.

FACING THE PAST

As we walked back to the car, my date's mouth was agape. "Why did you come if you knew Cindy and once made her cry?" she asked. I was too devastated to reply. Going in, I'd had no idea that something I'd said or done in third grade had left such a deep scar on Cindy.

The drive to my friend's house party was a blur of emotions. Surprisingly, one emotion I didn't feel was anger. At that point in my life, I was dealing with my family's very public legal troubles, including my father's arrest and the FBI's involvement. I was an angry teenager, quick to deflect blame onto others. But this time was different.

For the first time, I truly owned up to something I'd done. I realized that what I had considered a trivial childhood incident had left a lasting impact on Cindy. She had carried that pain for over ten years, and I deserved to know—even if the circumstances were harsh.

A CHANCE FOR HEALING

Fast forward five years. I was at a local bar with some friends when Cindy walked in with her friends. She came right up to me, and before she could say anything, I blurted out, "Cindy, I'm really sorry for everything. I don't know if I said it all and if it stuck the last time I saw you, but I feel terrible. I'm sorry!"

Cindy started to tear up and said, "I have felt bad every day since my sister's wake. While you did make me cry, I shouldn't have acted like that, and I'm sorry." We both smiled awkwardly, and I tried to lighten the mood with a laugh.

"That will go down as the most memorable first date wake experience of all time."

I never saw Cindy again after that night, but I'm glad we ran into each other. It gave both of us a chance to heal and move forward.

This story offers a powerful lesson about the lasting impact of our actions and words, particularly those we may have long forgotten but that others carry with them. We may not always understand the long-term effects of our past actions on others, but part of being Au Sm is rebuilding trust in our lives, even when it feels uncomfortable or unexpected

3

MAKE SOMEONE'S DAY

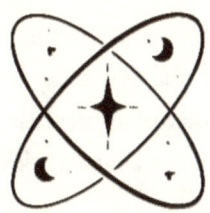

GRATITUDE

I OFTEN ASK A simple yet powerful question in my keynotes: "What if everyone made someone's day?"

It's a question I use to guide me as I strive to make someone's day every day. But it's not just about what I can do for others; I love sharing when someone makes my day.

One person who has made my day many times over the years is Kim Weis Laugherty. I've known Kim for over fifteen years, and she and her team at the Ohio Association of School Business Officials gave me a platform before my speaking career even began. In 2023, I had the honor of delivering their closing keynote, and afterward, I handed out stickers—a small token of appreciation and positivity.

As I was doing this, Kim turned to one of the attendees and said, "Mine goes everywhere with me." She pointed to a sticker I had given her a couple of years ago, now proudly displayed on her laptop. I hadn't noticed it at first, but when I did, it struck me. Seeing her smile and her pride in showing it made my day.

Even after all these years, I'm still blown away when I see people representing Be Au Sm. Kim, you made my day. Thank you for that.

THE RIPPLE EFFECT OF GRATITUDE

Kim's simple act of keeping a sticker on her laptop was more than a gesture—it was a powerful reminder of the impact we can have on one another. When we take the time to make someone's day, we spread positivity and joy. And when someone makes our day, it reminds us of the power of connection and the importance of appreciating those moments.

So the next time you have the chance, ask yourself: "What if everyone made someone's day?"

You might be surprised at the Au Sm ripple effect it creates.

4

WHAT ARE THE CHANCES

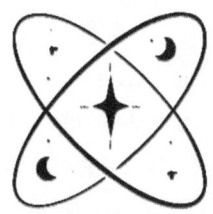

GRATITUDE

I MET PAUL ANASTASI as a client in 2004. We weren't close or even friends per se, but that changed in 2006 when I invited him to our annual customer conference. Paul was set to come, but a family death disrupted his plans, and the airline wouldn't let him reschedule. Rather than let him miss out entirely, I called American Airlines, impersonated Paul, and managed to change his flight to Wilmington, North Carolina. A bit further away from Myrtle Beach, but still manageable. I met him at the airport, and on the way to the car, I told Paul, "Good news, I got us a Jeep with no top."

"Oh, good," he sarcastically replied. "That'll work out great for my skin cancer treatment."

That car ride was the beginning of a beautiful friendship. We've taken hundreds more since then. Paul's one of my closest friends. He also happens to be the guy who saved my life.

A LIFE-SAVING MOMENT

On March 13, 2017, I delivered a keynote for the New Jersey School Building and Grounds Association (NJSBGA) in Atlantic City. I came down to the trade show floor afterward, absolutely starving, grabbed a beer and a prime rib sandwich, and dug in. That first bite was incredible. The second, though, was a different story.

As I tried to wolf down a fist-sized bite, it lodged right in my throat. My heart rate went haywire—I couldn't breathe, couldn't move. Paralyzed by fear, I couldn't even give the universal choking signal. Paul saw me and immediately realized something was wrong. He rushed over and performed the Heimlich maneuver twice (cracking two of my ribs in the process) but finally dislodged the steak. I could breathe again. Paul saved my life.

The paramedics arrived, checked my vitals via my Apple Watch, and insisted on taking me to the hospital. But all I could think about was getting home to Amy. Despite the risk, I signed the waiver to waive further treatment and left.

It was a shocking experience, no question, and everyone felt rattled. Finally, someone in the group asked, "What now? What should we do?"

"Let's go to the casino and have a drink," I said.

Within five hands, someone in our group won $5,000, but I had had enough. All I wanted was to go home, and I decided then and there to drive straight back to Massachusetts.

FROM GRATITUDE TO A MIRACLE

But life has a funny way of weaving stories together. It wasn't the first time I had almost died, but it was the first time I'd felt an urgent need to be with someone I loved. I went home to Amy, happy to be alive but also grateful for our relationship and the life we had built. That night was the first time I held her, wondering if it might have never happened had Paul not been there. Returning home was the right decision, one that led to another life-changing moment.

But first, let me give you the backstory, which began with a proposal.

On February 13, 2015 (yes, it had to be the 13th), I asked Amy to marry me, and she said yes. We were thrilled but quickly faced our share of challenges. A brutal polar vortex nearly destroyed our home that winter, causing $250,000 in damage. Almost a full year of repairs and endless setbacks tested us, followed by difficult news from the doctor that the chances of us having children were slim to none, as in fat chance or no chance.

For two years, our lives were a mess of house repairs and fertility struggles. In January 2017, we finally took a vacation to Mexico, just the two of us, and made the tough decision to let go of the idea of having kids and simply focus on appreciating the life we had together. It was a moment of pure gratitude for what we had, and I think that energy shifted something in both of us.

THE GREATEST GIFT

Crisscrossing the country for sales calls and speaking gigs is never easy. Whether the trips are planned or not—and the latter happens far too often—it adds another layer of stress and worry into a relationship.

An April 2017 trip to North Carolina was planned well in advance, but the timing was still difficult for Amy and me. We still had many unresolved issues with the home renovations, and Danny's schedule was busier than ever.

After my first meeting, I called home to say hi to Amy. I could sense something was off, but in a good way. That's when she told me about the pregnancy test. I was floored and caught the next flight home. On the way to the house, I stopped at Target and bought seven more pregnancy tests. With everything the doctors told us ("fat chance or no chance"), I wasn't sure what to think. But the tests were right.

On December 11, 2017, Chance was born.

Looking back, it's staggering how connected everything feels. After Paul's Aunt Jenny passed away in 2006, he told me he wouldn't attend our annual conference due to the airlines. Most people would have said, "No problem, I understand." But that's not what I said to him. I think my exact words were, "That's unacceptable. Let me see what I can do."

Paul became more than a client that day. That's why he was able to save my life years later and, unknowingly, set in motion the events that led to our son's birth. Maybe it's all coincidence. Maybe not. But this string of events has left me profoundly grateful—for Paul saving my life—and for every challenge that pushed Amy and me to be where we are now.

That's the funny thing about life: Sometimes, it's the seemingly unrelated moments that create the greatest gifts.

And Paul is unquestionably one of my life's greatest gifts.

5

TOUGH ACT TO FOLLOW

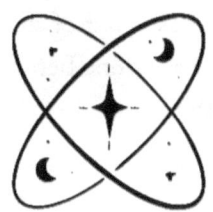

GRATITUDE

My first tradeshow in the software industry was in 1997. Turns out, that was Sharon Bruce's first industry show as executive director of the Connecticut ASBO (Association of School Business Officers). Our paths haven't stopped crossing since, and I'm the better person for it.

Sharon Bruce gave me my first speaking opportunity in this space. Remember how I had struggled to gain traction as a workshop presenter? Well, that drought ended in 1997 when Sharon invited me to address a hundred people at an executive leadership retreat at the Water's Edge Resort in Westbrook, CT.

Not only that, but she gave me a great time slot. I was the second-to-last session of the day. You never want to be the last one of the day because people are already thinking about the cocktail hour that follows. And after lunch, well, that's the worst slot. Or so I thought.

Turns out, the person speaking after lunch had nothing to worry about. The lights dimmed, the smoke machines turned on, and there were two large screens, one on either side of the stage. The speaker was Paul Martin, an Ironman and Olympian amputee athlete and author of One Man's Leg.

Oh shit. I had to follow this guy?

I was supposed to give a talk on "After Hours Use of School Buildings" but immediately threw my canned presentation out the window. After opening with, "Well, if that isn't a tough act to follow, I don't know what is," I went rogue and shared stories about my experiences with after-school use of buildings. I didn't knock it out of the park, but considering who I had to follow, I couldn't have done better, and more importantly, it cemented my friendship with Sharon.

RECIPROCITY

After the talk, I made a point to find Sharon and thank her. "If there's anything I can ever do for you, just say the word," I told her—and I meant it.

Since that event in 1997, I've spoken to one of her groups more than fifteen times and have continued to tailor each of my talks to the audience members sitting in front of me, not what the executives wanted me to push. I guess I ought to thank Paul Martin, too, because there was no way I would have made it as a speaker with what I intended to offer the audience after his performance.

My keynote career began in 2012, and by 2014, I was the Paul Martin of Sharon's event. That keynote will always be special. Thanks to Sharon's blessing, it was the first talk where I publicly thanked my grandparents—especially Lola, my grandmother—for everything they had done for me growing up and throughout my life. The smile on Lola's face is something I will never forget.

UNEXPECTED GIFT

A few years later, Sharon again asked me to speak to her members in Falmouth, Massachusetts. Amy and I had just found out we were pregnant with Chance, and Sharon was one of the first people to hear the news. The event was at the Sea Crest Beach Resort, so I took Amy and Danny with me.

On the first night, we saw Sharon sitting on the beach. When we got closer, we saw that she was knitting—knitting a baby blanket for Chance. I'll always be grateful to Sharon for giving me the chance to speak in 1997, but that's nothing compared to the gratitude I have for her friendship and love

6

MR. PEANUTS

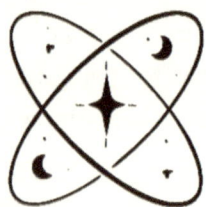

GRATITUDE

In October 2023, I welcomed Rodney Esser—or as most people affectionately called him, Mr. Peanuts—to the Midwest Facility Masters Conference. I created a video to introduce him to over four hundred attendees, and after everyone had left, I had the chance to sit down with him and learn even more about his incredible story.

For fifty-nine years, Mr. Peanuts has been a custodian at a public school district in Wisconsin. But during our conversation, I discovered that his impact went far beyond just cleaning. I learned about his early years, how he found his way to this role, and, most importantly, how he has dedicated his life to giving hope, love, and the cleanest, safest, and healthiest environment possible to the children in his care.

In a world where so many people struggle with their "why," Mr. Peanuts has it dialed in. He knows precisely why he does what he does. He pours his heart into it every single day—and has for six decades.

It's easy to take for granted the work of behind-the-scenes professionals. Not just custodians, but facility, kitchen, hospitality, operations, safety, and so many other workers. It's no exaggeration to call them unsung heroes in our communities.

Rodney Esser, Mr. Peanuts, is one of a kind. He is truly an Au Sm human being. In recognizing and appreciating his efforts, we honor every one of these heroes. They don't just keep our schools clean; they create environments where kids feel safe, valued, and cared for.

And that kind of impact lasts far beyond the school walls.

7

IT STARTED WITH A SHOUTOUT

GRATITUDE

ON APRIL 26, 2003, Aron Ralston found himself in a life-or-death situation that most of us could never imagine. During a solo descent of Bluejohn Canyon in southeastern Utah, he dislodged a boulder that pinned his right wrist to the side of the canyon wall. After five grueling days, Aron made the unimaginable decision to break his forearm, amputate it with a dull pocketknife, and then navigate through the rest of the canyon, rappel down a sixty-five-foot drop, and hike seven miles to safety.

This harrowing experience is documented in Aron's autobiography, *Between a Rock and a Hard Place*, and became the subject of the 2010 film *127 Hours*, where James Franco portrayed Aron. It's a story of survival, resilience, and the lengths one can go when faced with seemingly insurmountable obstacles.

AN UNLIKELY FRIENDSHIP

A little over ten years ago, I attended a dinner where Aron Ralston was the guest of honor. I didn't know Aron, but I'm not one to shy away from a bit of humor and a chance to connect. So, toward the end of dinner, I said, "Hey Ralston, tomorrow you're going to give a keynote to over a thousand people, and I could use some street cred. If you name-drop me, I'll take you out to the Office"—my childhood friend Greg's local bar—"and show you a great time with some awesome people."

To my surprise, Aron opened his keynote the next day with, "If someone named Peach invites you to go to the Office . . ." That moment sparked a friendship that has lasted years. Since then, I've had the honor of attending his keynotes several times. Aron shares powerful messages about turning your boulders into blessings, drawing from his harrowing 127-hour experience that changed his life. Aron's your guy if you're ever looking for a dynamic speaker with an incredible story.

THE ENERGY OF GRATITUDE

Reflecting on that story reminds me of the countless moments of gratitude I've experienced. In February 2024, I had my second 2:30 a.m. wake-up of the week to catch an early flight. On my hour-long drive to the airport, I thought about a question I always get: "How do you do what you do? Doesn't it exhaust you?"

My answer is always the same: "The people I have the honor to serve every day energize me, and I love that I get to wake up at 2:30 a.m. to see them—or to head home to see my family."

The truth is, I'm grateful every day for the work I do and the people I meet. Aron Ralston, my dad, my colleagues, and my family—each has shaped my journey in ways I can't fully express. Finding work you love with people you love is one of life's greatest blessings. Life is too short to spend forty-plus hours a week doing something that doesn't make you happy.

FINDING THE SILVER LINING

Aron's story reminds us that life is full of massive challenges—boulders, if you will. These boulders can seem daunting: depression, grief, addiction, divorce, loss. We all have them, and they can weigh us down and make it hard to move forward. But instead of focusing on what these boulders take from us, we can focus on what we still have. We need to appreciate the present, the opportunities in front of us, and the people around us.

We're all just people, but we have this extraordinary gift—life. Sometimes, we need to remove ourselves from the BS, the guilt, the excuses, and the blame. We need to stay focused on what we do have and be grateful for it. This doesn't mean settling for the status quo; it means recognizing the value in our experiences and using them to propel us forward.

Gratitude isn't just about being thankful for the good times. You must also find the silver lining in the challenges and appreciate the journey, no matter where it takes you. And when you live with gratitude, you'll find that life brings you exactly what you need, exactly when you need it.

Aron Ralston's story is about survival, resilience, and turning adversity into something positive. But for me, it's also a story of gratitude. I'm grateful for that dinner, the chance to connect with someone as inspiring as Aron, and the reminder that life's greatest rewards often come from unexpected places.

Every time I wake up at 2:30 a.m. to catch a flight, I remind myself how lucky I am to do what I do. The early mornings, the long hours, and the miles traveled are all worth it because I get to work with Au Sm people and come home to a family that means the world to me.

8

EMBRACING OUR CIRCUMSTANCES

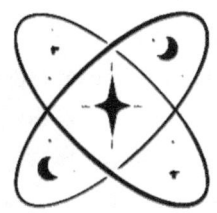

GRATITUDE

GRATITUDE HAS THE POWER to transform our perspective and elevate our lives, no matter the circumstances or fate we face. When I think about someone who embodies this transformative power, David Cooks immediately comes to mind. His story is one of incredible adversity but also one of strength, resilience, and an unwavering commitment to making the most of every day.

At the age of fifteen, David's life took a sudden and drastic turn. He experienced a spinal aneurysm that left him a T-6 paraplegic, confined to a wheelchair for the rest of his life. Almost in the blink of an eye, his world shifted from being a rising star in high school basketball to living in a rehabilitation facility, facing a lifetime of paralysis. For many, such a dramatic change would lead to despair, anger, and a sense of victimhood. But David chose a different path. Rather than succumbing to his circumstances, he accepted and embraced his new reality, determined to face life head-on.

TURNING CHALLENGES INTO PURPOSE

David's story has inspired people worldwide, and he shares it in his book Getting Undressed: From Paralysis to Purpose. The doctors kept telling him, at age fifteen, all the things he could no longer do. But David wasn't interested in what he couldn't do.

"As long as there's time on the clock, just do the best you can with what you have. I still had my arms," he told his family.

I first encountered David through LinkedIn. He had just launched his book, and I noticed we shared a mutual connection. Intrigued by his story, I ordered a copy of his book—but, as I've been known to do, I put it on the shelf without reading it right away.

A few months later, I was on a ferry boat to Nantucket, MA, with David's book in hand. I started to read it and was immediately captivated. I began marking the pages with thoughts and notes, feeling deeply connected to his story. I knew then that I had to meet him and have him on my podcast.

EMBRACING ADVERSITY

We eventually met at one of the busiest Starbucks in Madison, Wisconsin, and have been great friends ever since. What struck me the most about David is his gratitude for life, even in the face of overwhelming adversity. Like Aron Ralston, whose life changed in an instant with a boulder in Bluejohn Canyon, David's life was forever altered by his aneurysm. But neither man allowed their circumstances to define them. Instead, they focused on what they could control—their attitude, mindset, and, ultimately, their gratitude.

"It's not what happens to you; it's what you do with what happens to you," David often says.

And what David did was extraordinary. He took what many would see as an ending and turned it into a new beginning. He leveraged his situation to inspire others, becoming a successful businessman, writer, basketball coach, podcaster, and teacher. He didn't let his wheelchair confine his spirit or his potential. Instead, he used it as a platform to reach new heights.

SEEING THE OPPORTUNITIES

"Sometimes we miss opportunities looking for a different opportunity."

David Cooks

I love this line by David. It speaks directly to the heart of gratitude. It's easy to get caught up in what we've lost, in what we can't do, or in the opportunities that didn't come our way. But when we focus on what we still have, on the opportunities right in front of us, we begin to see the world differently. We start to appreciate the gifts we've been given, no matter how small they may seem.

David's story shows us that gratitude isn't about settling for the status quo. Instead, we should recognize the value in our current circumstances and use that recognition to fuel our growth. This requires understanding that while we may not have control over everything that happens to us, we do control how we respond. We can focus on what we have rather than what we lack. We can choose to be grateful for those moments that push us to grow, the setbacks that teach us resilience, and the opportunities that come from unexpected places.

LIVING WITH GRATITUDE

In a world that often emphasizes what we don't have, David Cooks stands as a beacon of what it means to live with gratitude. His life is a testament to the idea that when we embrace our circumstances with gratitude, we unlock a strength within ourselves that allows us to achieve greatness, no matter the obstacles in our path.

As you go through your day, remember David's story. Let it inspire you to focus on what you can control—your attitude, your mindset, and your gratitude. When you live with gratitude, you open yourself up to the extraordinary possibilities that life has to offer.

In the end, that's what being Au Sm is all about.

9

NO SECOND OPINION NEEDED

GRATITUDE

BEING A PUBLIC SPEAKER means you're almost always at the mercy of the booking organization's schedule. That's just part of the job. So when the opportunity to deliver a keynote in Wisconsin on Halloween in 2017 came up, I took it. I knew flying home after the talk to be with Danny and Amy for trick or treat was a gamble—with airline delays always a possibility—but fortunately, everything went smoothly. I made it home in plenty of time to enjoy the festivities.

That keynote was supposed to be my last big event of the year. For the first time in fourteen years with my company, I was taking an extended break from work to prepare for something far more important: Chance's arrival in December. Amy and I were preparing the house for a new baby, and work was no longer my top priority.

MEETING LES TRACHTMAN

I wasn't in the office the following day. Instead, I was logged in remotely for the big announcement: Our CEO, Kent Hudson, was stepping down, and Ed Roshitsh was taking over. I texted Kent after the call, and he said, "Do everything you can to help Ed succeed."

There was no hesitation on my part. I didn't know Ed yet, but being a team player has always been part of my DNA. A few months later, the company brought in Les Trachtman, an expert in transition leadership and the author of *Don't F**k It Up: How Founders and Their Successors Can Avoid the Cliches that Inhibit Growth.*

Some executives grumbled about having to read Les' book. Now, I'm not exactly a voracious reader (it did take me five years to graduate from high school), but if the executives had to read it, I figured I should too. Besides, the title spoke to me—it sounded like something I could learn from. And boy, did I.

Les and I eventually became close friends. Early on, I reached out to him on LinkedIn and set up a meeting. Despite his allegiance to the Mets (a sore point for this lifelong Red Sox fan), we hit it off immediately. Les quickly became a fan of Be Au Sm and my work. I even went to his house to record a podcast episode, and we bonded further over a Blue Angels show.

LOSING A JOB, FINDING A FRIEND

Looking back, meeting Les wasn't just a professional connection—it was one of the hidden blessings of that turbulent time.

Fast forward sixteen months: my company was sold. Then COVID-19 hit, and 140 people lost their jobs. In August, Ed left. By December, after seventeen years with the company, I was let go.

It hits hard when you're fired, especially after dedicating so many years to a company. I was the second-leading revenue driver at the time, but office politics and personality differences sealed my fate. Losing that job crushed my self-worth. It felt like everything I had worked for meant nothing. I was angry—at my employer, situation, and life. My dad was in a nursing home, battling dementia during the height of COVID. I was at one of the lowest points in my life.

But in the middle of all that chaos, there was Les. Minutes after I got fired, I called him. His first words? "Congratulations. We just happen to be hiring an evangelist."

Before I took the job, Les asked me to take a test—something all of his employees do before they get hired.

"I'll take it, but I want to give you the heads up, I don't really test that well," I told him.

"It's nothing to worry about, it's just something I have everyone take."

It turned out to be an intelligence test, but the good news (and shockingly, actually) was that it scored me as a genius! Other than Les's son, it was the highest IQ score he had seen within his company.

Twelve hours after losing a job I thought defined me, Les gave me a new opportunity. He believed in me when I wasn't sure I could believe in myself. Les didn't just help me financially; he kept me going emotionally. He reminded me that I wasn't just a tech salesperson but had something more to offer. And learning I was a "genius" despite not having a college degree? That was just proof that sometimes, the world sees more in us than we see in ourselves.

GRATEFUL FOR A SECOND CHANCE

Gratitude is about recognizing the people who step in when we need them most. Les did more than give me a job; he reinforced the importance of seeing the best in others. His belief in me validated the times I've tried to do the right thing for other people. When we make others feel valued and appreciated, we're creating something far bigger than a job or a moment—we're building legacies together.

I think about that moment when he answered my call and offered me a lifeline. That single act redefined my path. If there's one lesson I've taken from Les, it's this: Be the person who picks up the phone. Because you never know when your words, your faith, or your encouragement will be exactly what someone needs to move forward.

No second opinion needed here, Les—you've helped me live with G. R.A.C.E. from the moment we met.

RESILIENCE

RESILIENCE ISN'T ABOUT PRETENDING everything's fine. It's about what you do when things aren't fine—like facing disappointment, loss, failure, or life itself—and finding a way to stand back up.

For me, resilience has never been just a buzzword. It's been a way of survival. It carried me through the low points in my life, moments that nearly broke me. Resilience kept me moving forward—even when I didn't know where forward was.

Resilience isn't an automatic trait. Some days, the choice to be resilient was easy. Other days, it felt impossible. But every time we get back up, we prove to ourselves that we can. That's resilience.

This section doesn't cover theory alone—I share real moments that tested me, the kind that force you to decide whether you'll let life define you or whether you'll take control of your own story. Because the truth is, life doesn't care how many times you fall. It's up to you to decide how many times you get back up.

10

ANGRY AND ABANDONED

RESILIENCE

I'M A RELATIVELY HAPPY guy—but I'm not always Au Sm. I make sure to remind my audiences of that whenever I speak. The truth is, sometimes, the demons from our past catch up with us, no matter how far we think we've come. But since I've learned to live with G.R.A.C.E., those dark moments are fewer and further between.

This book is the first time I've shared my story in such detail. Confronting the past is never easy, but sometimes it's necessary if we want to move forward.

I wasn't born Joshua Peach. My last name—like my relationship with my biological father—didn't stick around very long. My mom, Ana, was married to him for five years before it ended. My biological father was a partner in one of the largest women's fitness salon chains, which were a huge deal in the 1970s and '80s. There were hundreds of them, and he made a fortune through that business.

By the time I turned one, my parents were separated. My father didn't even have the decency to call or tell my mom in person that he wanted a divorce. He had his secretary do it. This guy was not a good man. Despite his wealth, he sold our house and disappeared from our lives. He left my mom with nothing—no child support, no emotional support, not even a crib for me.

THE FIRST FATHER FIGURE

So, my mom and I moved in with my grandparents in West Bridgewater, MA. My mom was barely out of high school, raising me while also doing her best not to disappoint her parents. Life wasn't easy, and her job opportunities were limited.

Then, she got a big break: an offer to run her own fitness salon in Bridgeport, CT. It was an amazing opportunity, but it meant leaving me with her parents until she settled. It took three years. We talked on the phone every night, and she came home on weekends and one night during the week. But still, I spent those years being raised primarily by my grandparents.

My grandparents were Portuguese immigrants and factory workers who barely spoke English. Even though I was just a little kid, I became their translator to the outside world. My grandparents quickly became my best friends.

Finally, when I was about four, I moved back in with my mom in Bridgeport. Things were chaotic, but they felt a little more stable. Then, my mom met a police officer named JC. After about a year of dating, we moved into a condo together. And for a few years, I thought I had the father figure I'd always wanted.

ANOTHER ABANDONMENT

JC was a cop—someone to look up to. He taught me how to ride a bike and let me ride in his police motorcycle sidecar. I idolized him. He even adopted me, and I changed my last name to his. For the first time, I felt normal. I felt like I belonged somewhere.

But like my biological father, JC abandoned me too. After five years, he left us. I can't blame him entirely for the failed marriage, but that didn't erase the feeling of abandonment.

After the split, my mom and I moved to Easton, MA to be closer to her parents. JC promised me that "nothing would change" and that we'd still spend time together. But when I called him, he never answered. Eventually, the woman who picked up the phone said he wasn't there, and I got the same reply from his office. He didn't want to be part of my life anymore.

Two years later, he paid off his child support in one lump sum. With that money, my mom bought me new furniture for my bedroom. That was it—the end of my relationship with the man who had adopted me. I was in fifth grade, and I'll never forget how it felt to be written off like that, how it was all so transactional: new furniture in exchange for no longer having a father.

CONFRONTING THE ANGER

I was angry. Angry to the point where I wanted to hurt him. When I was twenty-five, I drove to a boatyard where he lived in Bridgeport. I had his old nightstick with me and was going to use it. I sat in the parking lot, fuming, replaying every moment of feelings of betrayal in my head. I thought it would help. I thought I'd feel better if I confronted him and made him feel my pain.

But I didn't do it.

I drove away instead, still filled with anger. How could someone who supposedly loved me walk away like that? I carried that anger for years. It ate away at me. I blamed myself. What had I done wrong? Why wasn't I good enough to keep him around?

It took me a long time to let go of that anger. To realize that it wasn't about me. That sometimes, people leave, and it has nothing to do with who we are.

Looking back now, I see those experiences for what they are: tests of my resilience. I had to find a way to keep going, to build myself up even when others had torn me down. I had to find my strength and, eventually, peace.

Resilience isn't just about surviving the blows you face; it's about refusing to let those blows define who you are. It's about finding a way to pick yourself up again and again, even when everything around you falls apart. I didn't have the dads I deserved, but I'm still here. And I've built a life I'm proud of, a life that's my own.

If you've been left behind or felt abandoned or written off, remember this: You are stronger than you think. You can get back up, no matter how many times you've been knocked down. That's resilience.

That's living with G.R.A.C.E.

11

WHEN WE DON'T FEEL AU SM

RESILIENCE

BELIEF IS A POWERFUL force. It's the foundation of how we see ourselves and navigate the world. But believing in yourself isn't always easy—especially when you don't feel Au Sm.

I learned that firsthand one summer at Stonehill College, where I spoke to a large group of kids at a summer camp. Speaking to middle and high school kids is no small feat. They can be a tough crowd—hard to reach and hard to connect with.

But the message I drill down in all my talks is simple: If you can be anything, be Au Sm.

At the end of every talk, I open the floor with a chance to "ask Peach anything." It's usually the fun, interactive part of the talk where the audience can ask whatever's on their minds. But that day, I got a question that completely caught me off guard.

A boy stood up and asked, "I'm not awesome. What do you do if you're not awesome?"

THE POWER OF CONNECTION

No one had ever asked me that before, and it hit me hard. But I was grateful for it because it was an opportunity to remind him—and everyone else in the room—of something incredibly important: I'm not always awesome, either. None of us are.

The first step in building resilience is believing in yourself, even when no one else does. Being Au Sm doesn't mean always feeling awesome—it's more about how you think about yourself and those around you.

Afterward, I made sure to find the boy. I handed him one of my "Be Au Sm" stickers for his Hydro Flask and gave him my phone number. I told him he could call me anytime, day or night. Later, I found out I had made an impression on him. The boy's father called me a couple of months after the talk. He said my message helped his son feel better. He was grateful.

THE LESSON IN BELIEF

Turns out, the boy was going through some really tough family and personal issues. No wonder he wasn't feeling awesome. Life was throwing more at him than any kid should have to deal with.

But that's the lesson here: We all go through things that make us feel less than Au Sm. We all have days where we're not sure if we're enough or if we'll ever make it through the hard stuff. Belief is the catalyst for greatness. It gives us the courage to face the hard stuff, process what's happening in our lives, and find our way through it.

RESILIENCE IS A CHOICE

This story is a reminder that believing in yourself is a daily choice. It's not always easy, and it doesn't always feel natural, but it's necessary. Also, resilience doesn't mean you have all the answers, but rather, you have the courage to face the questions. When you don't feel Au Sm, it's even more important to push ahead—knowing that every step forward is progress. And sometimes, it's about letting others help you when you're struggling to find that belief on your own.

We all need those reminders sometimes, don't we?

The next time you feel less than Au Sm, remind yourself that resilience is built one step, one belief, one moment at a time. And don't be afraid to share that belief with someone else who might need it. You never know how much one small act of encouragement can mean to someone else.

12

FINDING PEACE IN THE CHAOS

RESILIENCE

September 11, 2001, started like any other Tuesday. I woke up between 5 and 6 a.m., drove to my warehouse in Easton, and began my day. I had just moved back home with my parents after a relationship ended, and emotionally, I was going through the motions. My parents were dealing with their own struggles, too, so my days had become routine: get up, go to work, get things done, and repeat it all the next day.

Because it was early September, the truck and van were empty. In New England, we never loaded the night before if the temperature was over 60 degrees or under 32, so we always loaded in the morning. My dad helped me load the truck that day, and he took a couple dozen bottles to deliver to customers before heading out to play golf with some friends.

Usually, I started my delivery route at the furthest point and worked my way back, but that day, I did the opposite for some reason. It was a less efficient delivery method, but I didn't think much of it.

AN ORDINARY DELIVERY

My first stop was at the VA hospital. They were taking a lot of water, and while I was there, I talked with the girl I was planning to fly to Virginia Beach with on Friday. It felt like the perfect getaway. After my breakup, I hadn't dated anyone in months, and this was something to look forward to. Life was starting to feel a little brighter.

The next stop was the *Brockton Enterprise* on Main Street. It was a four-story building, and I had deliveries to make on each floor. When I made my first drop, the newsroom was its usual chaotic self—reporters at their desks, on the phone, chasing stories, and scheduling interviews. I often wondered how they did their job, especially since a bad experience with a reporter years earlier had left me with a poor impression of the profession.

THE WORLD CHANGES IN AN INSTANT

After finishing my first drop, I loaded more bottles and returned to the second floor. As I stepped out of the elevator, I noticed something was off. All the reporters were huddled around the TVs, and the usual buzz of the newsroom was replaced by silence. Focused on my job, I kept moving. Then, I heard a shriek.

I looked up at the TV and saw one of the Twin Towers engulfed in smoke. It didn't register at first—everything felt like it was moving in slow motion. I stood there, stunned, trying to process what I was seeing. I didn't quite understand the magnitude of what I had witnessed—I'm not sure anyone did—and, for some reason, I returned to delivering the water.

A few minutes later, another shriek rang out, followed by cries of "Oh my God!" I rushed back to the newsroom; this time, both towers were smoking, billowing with thick, dark clouds.

A LESSON IN RESILIENCE

September 11, 2001, began like any other day, but by the end of it, the routines of an entire nation were shattered. It tested everyone's resilience, forcing us to confront the uncertainty of life and how quickly things can change.

Whether dealing with the shock of a national tragedy or simply navigating the ups and downs in your everyday life, leaning into resilience helps keep you moving forward. Resilience isn't just about bouncing back from challenges—it's about facing them head-on and coming out stronger. To be resilient is to maintain your center, even when the world around you seems to be spiraling out of control.

It's because of resilience that we can find peace in the chaos.

13

THE FBI RAID

RESILIENCE

IN THIRD GRADE, MY mom and I moved back to Massachusetts after her divorce from JC, her second husband. She took a job at the Gloria Stevens Figure Salon Corporate Offices, wanting to be closer to my grandparents in West Bridgewater.

We moved into a condo at 13 Pinebrook Lane, a place worlds apart from our previous condo in Bridgeport, CT. Peaceful and quiet, it feltlike we were out in the middle of nowhere—exactly the escape my mom needed. The condo belonged to a man named Eric Peach. By fifth grade, Eric and my mom were a couple, and when they married, Eric became my father. I changed my last name to Peach, and he remains, to this day, the only one I call Dad.

THE FAMILY TALK

With multiple rental properties, Eric was hard-working and financially successful, but he didn't flaunt it. He kept things low-key, living in worn-out jeans, driving a Nissan Stanza, and wearing shoes often held together with electrical tape. We lived comfortably yet modestly. We'd stay in Motel 6s, eat at the Ground Round, and take trips to his parents' place in Cape Breton, Canada. In 1990, he and my mom started building their dream home behind our house. We moved in a year later, even though it wasn't fully finished. It was nice but unassuming—just like Eric. Life was stable, and for the first time, I felt like I had the security I'd always wanted.

But then, in 1992, my dad sat us down for a family talk. I was seventeen, a struggling student, and I had already repeated tenth grade. That night, my dad told us there was a "high probability" he would be indicted. I didn't even know what being indicted meant, but in simple terms, he explained he might go to jail because of something his company had done. I remember sitting there, stunned, thinking, this can't be real.

WHEN THE FBI CAME

There was a gap between that conversation and October 1st. I woke up that day like any other, ready to pick up friends for school. Walking to my car, I saw two Crown Victorias coming up our long driveway. The two vehicles held six men in suits. Surreal doesn't even cover it. With a driveway as long as ours, anyone driving up it was either expected or something was seriously wrong.

One of them asked, "Is Eric Peach home?"

"Yeah, he's upstairs, in bed."

They walked past me like I wasn't even there, straight upstairs to wake up my dad and arrest him. My dad asked for a moment to put on proper clothing, but they refused. He threw on his ripped jeans and a Canada tee, and the FBI escorted him right out of the house. On his way out, he looked at me and said, "Don't worry. Everything will be okay." And then he was gone. My mom thought it best I go to school and keep things as "normal" as possible, though nothing would ever feel normal again. Honestly, that was the last day of my adolescence as I knew it.

A FATHER'S DECISION

That night, Dad came home and pulled me aside. He told me that the FBI had charged him with sixty-nine counts of bank fraud. But the truth was, they didn't really want him—they wanted the people above him, higher-ups like politicians and top executives. He had an option: He could walk free if he provided evidence on these people. I'll never forget what he told me. "Josh," he said, "if you do something wrong, even if you didn't know it was wrong, it doesn't make it right." He chose to take responsibility for his actions, knowing the price he'd pay.

At least back then, with no internet, the news took a bit longer to circulate. But within a day, it was all over. His arrest was front-page news, and of course, my dad was the one in handcuffs, in his ripped jeans and Canada tee, plastered across every screen. Many friends turned against me. They called my dad a crook and worse. I felt alone and angry. My dad was going to jail, I was repeating tenth grade, and I felt like everyone I knew abandoned me.

True to his word, my dad didn't turn against the others, and the government seized everything—his assets, his accounts. He lost it all. He became a convicted felon, under house arrest, wearing an ankle bracelet. It was devastating, and in a small town, he was viewed as a criminal even after his sentence ended.

In 1995, he started a water business. He bought a used panel van and drove to western Massachusetts to pick up five-gallon bottles to sell. Slowly but surely, he built something new from the ground up.

FACING HARDSHIP

If I learned anything from my dad, it's that resilience means facing hardship, not running away from it. Life didn't stop for my dad when everything fell apart; it didn't stop for me, either. I had to carry on. This was resilience in its rawest form—facing each day despite the shame, hurt, and anger.

I'll never forget the day the FBI raided our home and arrested my dad. How could I? But I no longer carry the anger or resentment. Instead, what really stands out in my mind about that morning is the way my dad kept his head high—even when the world around him felt like it was crashing down.

Living your legacy isn't always easy or comfortable—but we always have a choice. Thank you, Mom and Dad, for showing me the way.

14

THE ST. PAUL SCRATCHER

RESILIENCE

THE NUMBER THIRTEEN HAS always held significance for my family. Friday the 13th marked the day my grandparents immigrated to the United States from Portugal. On February 13, 2015, I proposed to my fiancée, Amy, in what should have been the start of an exciting new chapter in our lives. But just a day later, as we prepared to celebrate Valentine's Day and our engagement, disaster struck.

Water flooded into our dining room from the ceiling. Ice dams, caused by the relentless Polar Vortex winter, had wreaked havoc on our home. Within 24 hours, we went from celebrating to watching our house being destroyed.

WHEN THE UNEXPECTED HAPPENS

Months later, our house was still in chaos. The renovation dragged on, delays from the mortgage company compounded the stress, and my finances were stretched thin. Then came a last-minute work trip to Minnesota. I wasn't eager to go, but the trip offered a brief escape from the financial and emotional drain of rebuilding our home.

At the Minneapolis-St. Paul airport, as I paced the gate, stressed about the mounting bills, I spotted a lottery ticket machine. On a whim, I bought a $20 scratch ticket. As I scratched the ticket while boarding, I discovered that I had matched number 28. Expecting a small win, I was stunned to see the prize: $10,000.

The timing couldn't have been more perfect. Just as I was about to lose hope, this unexpected windfall gave me the breathing room I desperately needed to keep going.

The story isn't about winning $10,000. More than just a lucky break, it was a reminder that even when life feels overwhelming, there's always a reason to keep moving forward. That ticket didn't solve all my problems, but it gave me something I needed in that moment: breathing room, a spark of possibility, and the energy to keep pushing through.

BELIEF FUELS RESILIENCE

Belief is powerful, but it's not enough on its own. Believing things can and will get better is essential, but we still have to show up, put in the work, and take action—especially when it feels like everything is stacked against us.

When I think back to that February, I realize it wasn't the lottery ticket that got us through; it was the resilience to keep going despite the chaos. The $10,000 was a momentary reprieve, but what mattered most was not giving up, even when the ceiling was literally crashing down around us.

Life will always have its floods, whether they're caused by ice dams or the storms we never see coming. What matters is how we respond—how we keep believing in better days while doing the hard work to make them happen.

So, when the unexpected happens—and it will—remember: Belief isn't a passive thing. It's what fuels your resilience. It's what keeps you moving forward when quitting feels easier. Believe in possibility, but don't let up. Put in the work, even when it feels impossible.

That's how brighter days come—not by chance, but by choice.

15

STEVE THE JERK

RESILIENCE

I RECENTLY FOUND MYSELF having a heart-to-heart with Steve the Jerk, our Be Au Sm mascot rooster. Steve was getting picked on by Igor, our Guinea Hen, and the bullying was clearly starting to wear him down. So, I decided to sit down and talk with Steve to share a few thoughts from my experiences.

As I watched Steve struggle with Igor, I couldn't help but think about times when people or situations tried to grind me down, chipping away at my confidence. We've all been there—dealing with those who seem determined to make our lives harder, who take up space in our heads and make us doubt ourselves. Whether it's a demanding boss, a toxic relationship, or even our negative self-talk, it's easy to let those things weigh us down.

I told Steve something my friend Scott Carpenter always reminds me of when I let people get under my skin:

"Illegitimi non carborundum."

It's a funny, made-up Latin phrase that means, "Don't let the bastards grind you down." It's a simple but powerful reminder that we can't give negative influences more time or space than they deserve.

We all face moments where we feel like we're being pecked at by life, where the small things or the bigger challenges start to eat away at us. But resilience isn't about avoiding those challenges. It's about facing them. When we let others—or even our own doubts—wear us down, we give them power they don't deserve.

Steve the Jerk may have been having a rough day, but with a bit of encouragement and a reminder to stay strong, he was ready to keep strutting confidently—and so can you.

So, if you're feeling like Steve the Jerk—if life has you down and people are trying to take up too much real estate in your mind—remember this: Don't let the bastards grind you down.

"Our ability to endure is always greater than our willingness to endure."

David Cooks

16

FUN OVER FEAR, ALL DAY LONG

RESILIENCE

I'VE HAD MY FAIR share of brushes with disaster—or at least what felt like disaster at the time. These moments, though terrifying, have taught me valuable lessons about resilience, perspective, and focusing on what you can control rather than the worst-case scenarios.

In 2008, I was in great shape. I had just finished a three-mile run on the treadmill, clocking in seven-minute miles, when I returned to my hotel room, fell asleep, and didn't wake up for twenty hours. When I finally came to, I was drenched in sweat and running a high fever. After flying home, I was admitted to the hospital, diagnosed with pneumonia, and pumped full of fluids.

What happened next blindsided me. The prescription I was given triggered an allergic reaction that caused temporary blindness. I was out of work for almost a month, and during a follow-up scan, doctors spotted a mass in my lungs. What followed were five agonizing months of tests and uncertainty. My weight climbed from 175 to over 200 pounds as depression crept in. I was consumed by the belief that I was dying.

Finally, the diagnosis came: sarcoidosis, an unexplained disease with three outcomes—it could disappear, stay the same, or kill you. There was no treatment, just observation. My mind latched onto the worst possibility. I spent months consumed by the thought that I was dying. That experience taught me my first real lesson in resilience: Fear grows when you feed it.

BRUSH WITH DISASTER

That wasn't the only brush with disaster. In 2012, I was electrocuted. That same year, after Hurricane Sandy, I was nearly struck by lightning. On March 13, 2017, I almost choked to death on a prime rib sandwich. Each time, I came face-to-face with how fragile life is—and how lucky I've been.

The most recent scare came in 2023 when I scheduled my first colonoscopy. At forty-eight, I was three years past the new recommended guidelines, which state you should get one at forty-five. "Am I early or late?" I wondered.

This time, I approached the experience differently. I had learned to let go of the fear and find humor in the process. When I called to schedule the appointment, I told the receptionist, "It's about damn time you called me!" Confused, she asked what I meant. "My doctor says there are two cancers you don't want to die from, and your office can prevent both. When can I come in?"

By the time I hung up, she was laughing. She said I was her best call in seven years.

HUMOR IN THE FACE OF FEAR

On the day of the procedure, I brought that same mindset with me. As the anesthesiologist prepared me for sedation, I couldn't resist a joke: "Before I count backward from ten, I just want to say—where you're about to go, no man has gone before. I love you all. Seven..." I was out before I hit six, but I was told the room erupted in laughter.

The results were sobering: seven masses of concern. I needed biopsies. The old me—the 2008 me—would have spiraled into panic, consumed by worst-case scenarios. But this time, I approached it differently. I reminded myself of what I'd learned over the years: worrying changes nothing except your mental and physical health.

Nine days later, the results came back clear. I was relieved, of course, but also grateful for the perspective I'd gained. Instead of letting fear take over, I stayed positive and proactive. I didn't waste those nine days in a mental spiral. I focused on what I could control.

RESILIENCE THROUGH PERSPECTIVE

Life's most challenging moments are often out of our control. Whether we're ready or not, a diagnosis, an accident, or a setback at work could happen. What we can control in those instances is how we respond.

When faced with uncertainty, letting your mind go to the darkest places is easy. Trust me, I've been there. But dwelling on the ninety-nine things that could go wrong won't change the outcome—it'll only drain your energy and happiness. Instead, focus on the things you can control—your mindset, your actions, and the support system you build around you.

That's not to say I don't worry anymore—I do. But I've learned to spend less time on the "what ifs" and more on the "what's next." What can I do right now to impact my life or someone else's positively? What steps can I take to keep moving forward, even when the path ahead feels uncertain?

We shouldn't ignore fear or pretend everything's fine. To be resilient, we must find humor when we can, seek perspective when needed, and focus on the present rather than the unknown. The next time you face uncomfortable news, take a deep breath and remind yourself that you've faced challenges before, and you've come through stronger.

And don't forget to laugh along the way—it might just save your life.

17

GETTING FIRED

RESILIENCE

GETTING FIRED ISN'T JUST a professional blow—it's personal. It makes you question your value, your decisions, and your future. But every time I've been fired, I've ended up exactly where I was meant to be.

After graduating from high school in five years, I gave community college a chance. I dropped out in 1997—it wasn't working out. I was okay with my decision, but fortunately, I still had people who believed in me and my potential. Two of those people were my friend Chris's parents, Karen and Bruno Martignetti, a.k.a. Big B and Special K.

Big B introduced me to one of his tenants, who owned a cell phone business. On my first day, my new boss plopped a giant phone book on my desk.

"Start at the beginning and don't stop until you reach the end."

It wasn't the sales dream I had imagined, but I adapted. I quickly learned that if I cared for my customers, they'd send me referrals, which meant less time with that phone book.

That philosophy turned out to be my sales superpower and led to my first "real" job.

One day, Bob Bogardus called the store, desperate for a phone. I stayed late to make the sale, earning just $13 in commission. But Bob was impressed by my willingness to go above and beyond.

"Why did you stay open late for me?" he asked.

"Because if I take good care of my customers, they'll send me more customers," I told him.

"Would you be interested in a job?" he asked.

And just like that, I transitioned into software sales.

FIRED THE FIRST TIME

I was 22 when Bob hired me, and the opportunity felt like a huge step forward. I poured everything I had into the job. But by May 1998, something felt off. We were heading to a conference in New Hampshire, and Bob, usually upbeat and chatty, was unusually quiet. By the end of the day, as we walked to the car, I finally asked, "Bob, you're going to fire me, aren't you?"

"I'm fighting for you, but it doesn't look good," he said.

The next day, I turned in my laptop and credentials. I got two weeks' severance and three months of insurance. I was okay. I appreciated the opportunity and knew if I could land that job, I could find another. Bob even told me, "If another opportunity comes up, you'll be the first person I call."

THE NEXT CHAPTER

In April 2004, Bob called me with a new opportunity at Kent Hudson's company, SD.

"That's the stupidest name I've ever heard," I told him.

But I put on a suit, met with Kent, and became employee #13 at the company. Kent's pitch was simple: "Give me 30 days, and I'll give you 30 years. I'll give you fun, fame, and fortune."

I spent the next 16 years at SD. After Kent left and a private equity firm took over, the company culture had shifted. It became all about churn-and-burn—raising prices without adding value, focusing only on revenue. I was burnt out and angry. When COVID hit, I was feeling good about my side hustle, *Be Au Sm*, but less and less connected to SD.

In December 2020, I was let go. It happened quickly and without much explanation. By 5:01 p.m., I was shut off from everything—email, systems, and communication.

In Chapter 7 (*No Second Opinion Needed*), I introduced you to Les Trachtman, the person responsible for redirecting me toward something better—and reaffirming the value of resilience through relationships.

RELATIONSHIPS MATTER

Every firing, while a huge setback, has been a turning point rather than an ending. It's taught me to look beyond the immediate hurt and focus on the opportunities that follow. Each time, I've found my way forward—not by luck, but through resilience, relationships, and a belief in what I bring to the table.

When I got fired in 1998, it felt like the biggest setback of my life. But it was also the first time I realized that losing a job doesn't mean losing your worth. It's an opportunity to reassess, to adapt, and to grow. Bob's call in

2004 proved that being let go doesn't mean you're forgotten—it means you're being redirected.

By the time I was let go in 2020, I was ready. Sure, it still hurt. But I knew it wasn't the end.

Instead of moping around and feeling sorry for myself, I leaned in and trusted my instincts, relationships, and potential. That's what led me to where I am today, doing work I love and living life on my own terms.

If there's one thing I'd tell anyone facing a setback, it's this: **It's okay to feel the loss, but don't let it define you.** Focus on what you've learned, keep your relationships strong, and remember that every ending opens the door to something new. It's not about bouncing back; it's about building forward.

And if you're lucky enough to have people like Big B, Bob, and Les in your life, thank them—and make sure to be that person for someone else. Resilience is more than how you overcome challenges; it's also how you help others navigate theirs.

18

THERE ARE NO GUARANTEES

RESILIENCE

It was the Saturday after Thanksgiving, November 26, 2022. My mother and grandmother were hosting a Portuguese festa with Portuguese steak on a stick, rolls, and other great food. We were supposed to be there around 4 p.m.

At 3:56 p.m., knowing we would be late, I saw Chance decorating the Christmas tree by himself, which he wasn't supposed to be doing. I couldn't help but take a picture and send it to my mother, letting her know we would be a few minutes late.

I put my phone down, but at that exact moment, my mother sent me a picture of my grandmother Lola sweeping the deck, preparing for our arrival.

As was my habit, I also had the police scanner on. Some people might find that odd, but it connected me to what was happening in my town. Then, I heard the call come through: "100-year-old not breathing."

My first thought was, How many 100-year-olds are there in my town? Time froze for a second.

Then, at 4:01, a text came through from my mom: "I think Lola had a stroke."

Even though she suffered from dementia, my grandmother was still sharp enough to know we were coming over for a celebration. Unfortunately, the voice on the scanner was talking about my Lola—only it wasn't a stroke; it was a brain hemorrhage.

"You need to come to the hospital to say goodbye," my mom said when she called a bit later.

I jumped into my pickup truck and sped to the hospital, driving 100 miles per hour down the highway. I remember thinking, What am I doing? Why am I listening to Christmas music? It felt so out of place. My grandmother was dying, and cheerful songs about Santa and reindeer filled the car.

I hit the scan button on the radio, trying to find something that fit the moment. As I did, I heard a voice on the radio say, "You die twice—once when you die, and once when they stop talking about you." It was Macklemore, a voice I hadn't heard in years.

"Be glorious," he said.

I doubt I will ever stop talking about Lola.

RESILIENCE IN THE FACE OF LOSS

My grandmother lived to be 100, a milestone that always made me think I had all the time in the world, just like her. She was my primary caretaker (and my best friend) during my formative years while my mom worked hard to provide for me. I thought we had more time together.

But in that moment, rushing off to the hospital to say goodbye, I realized just how wrong I was.

Nothing is guaranteed.

In my younger years, both in my personal life and my career, I was often reckless and out of control. I didn't think much about the future or how my actions might have consequences later. I wasn't always Au Sm. And to be honest, I'm still not. I'm a work in progress, just like everyone else.

Losing someone important to you is never easy, but resilience allows you to hold onto the good memories and push through the pain. When I think about my grandmother's life—her strength, her kindness, her unwavering care—I'm reminded that resilience is what carried her through 100 years. She didn't just survive; she thrived.

Life has a way of surprising you—one minute, you're watching your son decorate the Christmas tree; the next, you're rushing to the hospital to say goodbye to someone you cherish. Those moments remind us of life's fragility but also its beauty.

Lola's legacy has nothing to do with living to 100. Her legacy is the thousands of small actions she took that nobody ever saw, but everyone felt. The quiet preparations for a celebration. The way she made sure I had the basics while under her care as a toddler. The sacrifices she made without recognition. Her tireless commitment to her family.

I believe that resilience isn't just a personal trait—it's a gift we pass on. Every act of kindness, every bit of strength we show in tough times, becomes part of someone else's foundation. My grandmother gave me that gift, and I hope to pass it to Danny and Chance, and those who need it most.

Every time I catch myself hesitating—putting something off, convincing myself it can wait another day—I think of Lola sweeping the deck, preparing with quiet purpose. And then I remind myself: we don't get to choose how much time we have, but we do get to choose how we use it.

That's the kind of legacy I strive to live and honor every day.

ACTION

IDEAS ARE GREAT. PLANS are helpful. But at some point, you have to get out of your head and take action.

For the longest time, I thought action meant waiting for the right time—the perfect moment when everything would fall into place. But that changed when I started living my legacy. Action separates people who dream from people who make things happen. It can turn a thought into a movement, a challenge into an opportunity, and a moment into a legacy.

Otherwise, Be Au Sm wouldn't exist. My speaking career wouldn't have started. The moments that changed my life—the ones that led to new opportunities, relationships, and lessons—wouldn't have happened.

That's what this section is about. Taking the shot. Making the call. Getting off the sidelines and into the game. Because, at the end of the day, action is what creates impact. And once you take that first step, every step after gets easier.

19

THE START OF BE AU SM

ACTION

MY FIRST MOTIVATIONAL TALK was in 2012 at Gillette Stadium for an SD conference. The title of my talk was "To Change or Not to Change," and it was supposed to be a thinly veiled sales pitch. About 150 people were expected in the room, and let's be honest—it wasn't exactly the kind of thing to make me leap out of bed with excitement.

Three days before the talk, at Amy's birthday party, I was carrying Rooi, our 160-pound South African Boerboel, down the stairs. She had just had surgery and was terrified of balloons. When one popped nearby, she freaked out and tried to leap out of my arms. I held onto her for dear life, but we both tumbled down the stairs. I hit my head on the corner of the pool table and knocked myself out cold.

When I came to, the first thing I saw was my grandfather's old black metal suitcase sitting at the bottom of the stairs. That suitcase has always reminded me of what my family sacrificed when they immigrated to the

United States from Madeira. My grandfather brought his family here in 1966 with that single suitcase and a dream to create a better life.

Two days after the fall, still a little dazed, Amy looked at me and said, "What are you going to do for your talk? You can't back out now." She was right—I couldn't.

I also knew that I couldn't let this talk be some boring corporate sales pitch. It had to mean something. I threw out the sixty-two-slide deck of canned bullshit and rewrote the entire presentation around my grandfather and his story. "To Change or Not to Change" was no longer about selling anything. It was about the power of change and the sacrifices people make to create opportunities for others.

THE SUITCASE THAT STARTED IT ALL

On the day of the presentation, my bosses assumed I'd be giving the usual sales pitch. I didn't tell them I'd scrapped it. As I stood on that stage at Gillette, I talked about change in a deeply personal way, opening up about how my grandfather's courage to pack up his life and move to a new country gave me opportunities he never dreamed of. There were no guarantees for him, no safety net—just a suitcase and a belief that things could be better.

That talk was the beginning of something I hadn't planned for but immediately felt. The audience connected with my story, and before I knew it, I had three more speaking invitations. They weren't paid gigs, but I didn't care. For the first time, I saw a future for myself as a speaker, and it wasn't just about selling for my company anymore—it was about making an impact.

A $3 JOURNAL AND THE START OF BE AU SM

Fast-forward to 2015. Life wasn't great. That was the winter when the polar vortex tore through New England, causing all that damage to our home. Months of dealing with contractors, insurance adjusters, and endless stress had left me completely drained. I had another keynote scheduled for June, but I dreaded it. I didn't feel like I had anything left to give.

On the morning of the talk, a colleague handed me a book. It was actually a journal, and on the front cover were the words "Wake Up and Be Awesome." I thanked him, but he shrugged it off.

"Don't thank me too much—it was $3, and I got it at Target."

That journal might as well have cost $1,000 because it was exactly what I needed. I started jotting down ideas and reflections, which reignited something inside me. That $3 gesture was the unintentional spark that became Be Au Sm.

Sometimes, action doesn't come from some preconceived plan but from a simple nudge at just the right time.

ENTER ED ROSHITSH: A TURNING POINT

In 2017, everything changed when I met Ed Roshitsh, the new CEO of SD. I didn't know much about him initially, but Kent, our outgoing CEO, had handpicked him. When Ed and I first connected, I was struck by his directness and vision. Before our initial phone call ended, I ordered a copy of his book, A Solid Handshake.

Reading his book gave me a glimpse into his leadership philosophy, and it wasn't long before we started having deeper conversations.

"Why are you so committed to SD?" he asked me.

That question stuck with me. It made me think about my purpose, not just my job.

By June 2018, Ed had become more than a CEO to me—he was a mentor, a sounding board, and someone who believed in what I could accomplish beyond my current role. On the morning of June 19, 2018, Ed called me after finishing a twenty-mile run.

"I've got it!" he said excitedly.

"Got what?" I replied.

"The name of your book: Be Au Sm: The Essential Elements to Kicking Ass."

In that moment, something clicked. After we hung up, I didn't hesitate. I went straight to Legal Zoom and created the LLC for Be Au Sm. It was the first time I'd made a deliberate, intentional decision about a business idea. I'd always had tons of ideas, but I rarely acted on them. This time was different.

That same evening, I stood in front of 50 executive directors for state ASBOs at the Broadmoor Hotel in Colorado Springs, CO, and announced that my LLC had been created. I returned home and immediately landed my first two Be Au Sm keynotes, from two Au Sm individuals: Mike Haynes and Jeni Mather.

Mike's a childhood friend and owner of The Haynes Group, one of the area's largest commercial construction companies. He was an early supporter of Be Au Sm and still is. Jeni owns JM Pet Resort. She doesn't just treat the Peach family dogs and cats, she cares for them as if they were her own. You never forget your first gigs and the people who made them possible, so thank you, again, Mike and Jeni.

Things exploded from there. The following year, 2019, I did twenty keynotes. Just under sixty keynotes were booked for 2020, but I only completed twenty-one of them before COVID hit and the world shut down.

ACTION CREATES OPPORTUNITY

Some of the greatest opportunities in life come when you take action. Whether it's a spontaneous leap or a carefully considered move, action sets things in motion.

For me, action has meant taking risks, trusting my instincts, and learning from people like Ed Roshitsh, who saw more in me than I saw in myself. It's meant turning a $3 journal into a life-changing idea, scrapping a canned presentation to tell a meaningful story, and creating an LLC in one decisive moment.

Action isn't always easy. It's uncomfortable. It's uncertain. But it's also the catalyst for growth, change, and the legacy we leave behind. My grandfather's suitcase reminds me every day that my life is the result of someone else's courageous actions.

Living with G.R.A.C.E. means embracing action as the engine of change. It's not about having a perfect plan—it's about showing up, stepping up, and trusting the process.

So, what action will you take today? Whether big or small, deliberate or impulsive, your next move could be the start of something extraordinary.

20

WHY I ALWAYS GIVE MY HOME NUMBER

ACTION

IN 1997, I GOT my first set of business cards. I had just started working at ACT Software. Barely a month into the job, I already faced my first big challenge: I was asked to present in front of the entire company—a room full of people with college degrees and sales experience. I didn't have either.

Yet, when it was my turn, I knocked it out of the park.

After the presentation, management handed me my new business cards. My title was Account Manager, which apparently didn't sit well with some of the more seasoned employees. They didn't think the "new kid" deserved the same title as them, especially someone with no real-world sales experience.

Their complaints reached management, and a few weeks later, they took my cards away. When I got them back, my title had been downgraded to Junior Account Manager. I was furious.

TAKING ACTION

Instead of wallowing in frustration, I went to Quick Print in Easton, a local print shop where I once worked part-time. I asked the owner to create a new set of business cards but with a twist.

First, I removed the job title altogether. Instead of "Junior Account Manager" or "Account Manager," my card simply read: **Joshua Peach,** *At Your Service*

Second, I left off the company's 800 number and replaced it with my home phone number. I've done this for every business card since.

People always ask me why. The answer is simple: I want to be available to my customers when they need me, not just when it's convenient for me.

The truth is, hardly anyone ever calls my home number. But including it on my card sends a clear message: *I CARE.* That small action helped me stand out then and still does now.

IT'S THE MESSAGE, NOT THE MEDIUM

Today, most communication happens through cell phones, email, and social media. Even now, I still include my home number on social media posts and share it after keynotes. Not because I expect a flood of calls, but because it's a symbolic action—a gesture that says, "I'm still here for you."

The cards I printed in 1997 had no title because I didn't want my job to define me. My focus wasn't on climbing the corporate ladder or protecting my ego but on serving my customers. That mindset became the foundation of my career and remains central to everything I do.

AUTHENTIC ACTIONS MATTER

I'm not suggesting you put your home number on your business cards or social media posts. But I am suggesting you think about what actions you can take to differentiate yourself. The key is to be genuine, not gimmicky. People can sense the difference.

For me, it's the little things: responding quickly, admitting mistakes, and not worrying too much about spelling or grammar errors in my posts. I'm not trying to present myself as perfect or polished; I'm just showing up as my authentic self.

What actions can you take to show your customers, colleagues, or even friends that you care? Maybe it's being accessible in a way that feels personal. Perhaps it's focusing on service rather than sales. Or maybe it's simply taking time to listen.

Whether adding a home number to your business card or going out of your way to make someone feel valued, those actions speak louder than any title on a piece of cardstock ever could.

So take action. Not for the accolades but because it's the right thing to do.

21

HOW I BECAME FRIENDS WITH SANTA CLAUS

ACTION

In 2018, ED ROSHITSH pushed me to act on an idea I'd been toying with for years: creating a podcast. The goal was simple—to cast a wider net beyond my speaking events and share stories of people filled with purpose and passion who are doing truly Au Sm things.

I launched the Be Au Sm podcast in June 2018. Back then, podcasts weren't as ubiquitous as they are today—there were only about 600,000 shows compared to the 4.2 million now. People like Joe Rogan were starting to blow up, and I thought, "Why not me?"

But starting something new is never easy. After recording my second episode, I sat in my backyard under my peach tree and said to Amy, "Man, I suck at this. It feels so boring."

Amy, never one to let me wallow, replied, "Maybe you need guests."

"That's a great idea," I said. "But where am I going to find them?"

Amy just laughed. "Josh, you're on the road all the time and meet people everywhere. I'm sure you can find some great guests."

FINDING SANTA IN THE NORTH POLE

The next day, I had a crazy idea. I remembered hearing about a man who legally changed his name to Santa Claus and lived in North Pole, Alaska. He had to have an interesting story, right?

So, I called the North Pole Town Hall and asked for Santa Claus. The woman on the phone flatly said, "He's not here."

"He must be in the toy shop with the elves, getting ready for Christmas!" I joked.

Crickets.

After recovering from the awkward silence, I asked how I could contact him. She gave me an email address, which I emailed and got no reply. Then I called and left a voicemail—still nothing. Undeterred, I called again, leaving my number this time. And finally, Santa called me back.

At first, he was hesitant about appearing on the podcast. Santa had some political stances he believed might be too controversial, and he worried it could hurt my reputation. But as we talked, he opened up, sharing bits of his incredible story. By the end of the call, I had convinced him to let me visit him at North Pole City Hall later that month.

SANTA'S STORY AND IMPACT

Santa Claus—a former Special Assistant to the Deputy Police Commissioner of New York City (NYPD)—had spent much of his life advocating for vulnerable and underserved children. But how did he become Santa?

It started while he was a clergyman, living at Lake Tahoe, Nevada. He decided to grow a beard in 2004. It grew out completely white; and suddenly, everywhere he went, people started calling him Santa. He embraced it, volunteering as Santa for local charities and Nevada's Governor.

One morning while hiking through the snow and ice up in the mountains surrounding Lake Tahoe, he paused for prayer. He asked God if he should change his name to Santa Claus, making it easier to reach legislators throughout the country to advocate for child health, safety, and welfare.

Moments after his prayer, a white car drove by, and a young man inside shouted, "Santa, I love you!"

That was his sign. He applied for, and received, a court-ordered name change to Santa Claus. Then, he packed up and moved to North Pole, Alaska. He is in his third term as a North Pole City Councilman, currently Mayor Pro Tem, serves on the Executive Committee of the Sierra Club's Alaska Chapter, and continues his volunteer child advocacy online.

Santa appeared on *Be Au Sm* Episode 3, and we discussed his child advocacy for children who are abused, neglected, exploited, abandoned, homeless, institutionalized, and/or in foster care. He shared sobering statistics--more than three million children, that's one in thirty, in the United States fall into one of those categories.

To put that in perspective, the average classroom size is twenty-four children. So, when we send our kids to school, there is about an 80 percent chance that one of those kids is in each of those classrooms. The conversation was a real eye-opener for me and made me realize that we all need to step up and do more for our children.

When not helping children, he served as a city councilor, was president of the Chamber of Commerce, and even ran for United States Congress and president.

RECEIVING THE SUIT

Over the years, Santa became a regular on the podcast and a close friend. Together, we've raised money for Fairbanks Youth Advocates, a charity helping at-risk teens, and the Sierra Club's Alaska Chapter.

In December 2023, Santa called with a surprising announcement. "Josh, bring an extra suitcase on your next visit."

"*Why?*" I asked.

"Josh, I'm 77 years old, I've managed to lose a hundred pounds, and this is the last year I will be wearing my Santa suit."

Speechless doesn't even begin to cover it.

In July 2024, I flew to Fairbanks with a friend. Santa gave us a tour of his world in North Pole: the first cabin he lived in, where he worked as Senior Park Ranger his first two summers there, and even the diner where I'd had a reindeer omelet during my first visit in 2018. The final stop was his modest apartment, where he handed me his Santa suit.

I was overwhelmed. It wasn't just the suit itself--it was what it symbolized: Santa's belief in me, our friendship, and the shared mission to bring more goodness into the world.

Today, I'm the only person in the world who owns the Santa suit worn by the only man legally named Santa Claus ever to live in North Pole, Alaska. And it all started with a cold outreach for a podcast guest.

The suit is incredible, but what I love the most about Santa is his blessing: "May you enjoy a lifetime filled with happiness, peace, good health, prosperity, and, most of all, love—the greatest gift."

In other words, live your legacy--with love.

22

CHARTING YOUR OWN COURSE

ACTION

MARCH 2018 WAS A turning point in my career at SD. Our annual conference was held in San Diego that year, bringing together five hundred of our customers and prospects. As the company evangelist, I found this event to be as big as it got. It was my fourteenth conference and my fourth as a key presenter. Or so I thought.

Not that year.

Despite my role as one of the company's top revenue producers and a visible ambassador for our brand, I was abruptly sidelined. Two of SD's leaders had decided that my presence wasn't needed. They took it to the extreme: Not only did I have no speaking role, but I wasn't even listed as an attendee. I was completely shut out.

Thirty seconds after learning this, I made a decision. I wasn't going to sit this one out. Without hesitation, I booked a flight to San Diego and chartered the largest yacht in the harbor—all on my dime. It cost me $5,000, but I believed so deeply in this event, my ability to make an impact, and the potential to drive meaningful business outcomes that I didn't think twice.

A SUNSET ON THE HARBOR

The yacht was more than just a bold move—it was my way of taking control of a situation I refused to let define me. I invited three of my biggest prospects, Ed Roshitsh and his wife Christine, and one of our corporate partners to join me for a sunset cruise on the harbor. My goal was clear: I wanted to influence $200,000 worth of business by landing these three key accounts.

The stakes were high, but so was my commitment. For the evening, I engaged each prospect, addressing their concerns and painting a vision of what working with SD could mean for their organizations. By the night's end, all three prospects were on board—not just with the yacht but with SD.

The result? A new $200,000 worth of new business for the company, which more than paid for the cost of the yacht. But the impact went far beyond that.

For most of the evening, I found myself deep in conversation with Ed and Christine about my vision for Be Au Sm—the book, the speaking, all of it. At that point, I had only known Ed for four months, but his encouragement and insights that night became the spark that would ignite everything I've built since.

A CATALYST FOR CHANGE

That yacht was a bold statement. I could have let internal politics keep me on the sidelines. I could have sulked, complained, or waited for someone to recognize my value. But instead, I took action. I invested in myself and my vision because I knew sitting still wasn't an option.

That night in San Diego became the catalyst for launching Be Au Sm. It proved that sometimes, when the odds are against you, the only solution is to chart your own course. Taking that risk didn't just result in business wins, but it also gave me the clarity and confidence to pursue my goals, even when others doubted me.

CONTROL YOUR DESTINY

Life will put countless obstacles in your path—doubters, politics, and rejections. But action is what separates the dreamers from the doers. You might not have the resources to charter a yacht, but you can always take control of your circumstances and chart your path to success.

We control our destinies through the choices we make and the actions we take. Sometimes, those actions require risk, sacrifice, and putting yourself out there in uncomfortable ways. But every bold move you make is a step toward shaping the future you want.

When I look back at that night, I'm reminded that it wasn't about the yacht or the $200,000 in business. It was about refusing to let someone else decide my worth or dictate my role. It was about proving to myself and others that I could take the reins of my life and steer it in the desired direction.

What bold action can you take today to move closer to your goals? It doesn't have to be extravagant, but it does have to be intentional. The future you desire can only happen when you take action.

23

THE GATEWAY TO MAKING A DIFFERENCE

ACTION

In May 2019, Jamie Bender (a.k.a. Bender) and I were leaving the Alabama ASBO conference. It happened to be Cinco de Mayo, and we had an hour-long drive to the tiny Pensacola Airport. Upon arrival, we learned that our American Airlines flight was delayed. The weather was fine in Alabama, but thunderstorms had disrupted flights across the region.

Like everyone else, we were flying to another major airport to connect to the last leg of our trip home. With no direct flights out of Pensacola, every delay meant potentially missing our connections. After grabbing some food and drinks, we returned to the gate to find the delay had grown even longer. Frustrations were boiling over.

MEETING CATHY W.

Cathy W. was the gate agent that day, and she bore the brunt of the passengers' frustrations. People were hurling insults and complaints her way. "I'm never flying American again!" one passenger shouted.

Cathy, however, stayed calm and professional. "I understand your frustrations, but I can't control the weather," she said, repeating herself over and over as tensions rose.

One man in particular was being particularly obnoxious, playing the part of a big shot. His shouting was making Cathy's already impossible job even harder. I leaned over to him and whispered, "Hey, these people are trying their best. The more you yell, the less likely we'll get out of here. If you can tone it down, it'll help everyone." To his credit, he quieted down.

TAKING ACTION

Then, something surprising happened. A plane arrived early, catching everyone—including Cathy—off guard. The only problem? There was no ground crew to guide the plane to the gate. The fluorescent flag waver was missing.

I looked over to the gate, and Cathy was gone. A moment later, I saw her sprinting down the jet bridge. Seconds later, there she was on the tarmac, wearing a fluorescent vest and waving flags to guide the plane in herself.

It was over 100 degrees outside, and Cathy had just spent two hours fielding insults and frustration from passengers. Yet, instead of retreating, she ran straight into action—literally. She stepped far outside her job description because it was the right thing to do.

Once the plane was parked, Cathy sprinted back to the gate, a little winded but determined. She reopened the boarding process and checked us in with the same professionalism she'd shown all day.

ABOVE AND BEYOND

Thanks to Cathy's actions, we made our flight and, against all odds, our connections. For me, it was the difference between spending another night in an airport and making it home to my family. Her willingness to step up and do what was needed made all the difference.

Taking action—especially in the face of adversity—requires stepping up, stepping out, and sometimes, stepping far beyond what's expected of us. Cathy didn't just guide a plane in that day—she guided hundreds of us home.

When I saw her again two years later, I gave her a hug and said, "You saved my trip that day." She smiled and shrugged as if to say it was no big deal. But it was a big deal—to me and to everyone else she helped that day.

Cathy W. reminds me of why I end every podcast the same way: "If you can be anything, be Au Sm." Because when we show up like Cathy—with kindness, perseverance, and the drive to do what's right—we don't just do our jobs; we make a real difference in the lives of others. That's what it means to take action.

And that's what it means to Be Au Sm.

24

GET OUT OF THE CAR

ACTION

IT WAS A TYPICAL weekday morning. I had just dropped Chance off at school and was sitting in my truck, ready to head home. That's when I noticed him: an older man wearing a 101st Airborne Division T-shirt. Something about that shirt stopped me. My dad, Eric Peach, flew helicopters in Vietnam, and the 101st Airborne was part of his story. Without much thought, I got out of my truck, walked up to him, and introduced myself.

"Excuse me, I see you're wearing the 101st colors. Did you serve?"

He did. His name was Mr. Anderson, and the moment I mentioned my father, his face lit up. "Eric Peach? I know him well," he said with genuine warmth.

What followed was one of the most incredible conversations of my life.

LEARNING ABOUT MY DAD

According to Mr. Anderson, my dad flew him in and out of combat many times. He described my dad as one of the most commended service members he had ever known. While my dad never talked about Vietnam, Mr. Anderson shared details I'd never heard before—stories of bravery and recognition that filled me with awe. My dad had received commendations, including distinctions like the Distinguished Flying Cross and the Air Medal, though we didn't discuss specifics.

I was blown away. My father had locked his Vietnam experiences in a vault, and I had never felt entitled to open it. But here was someone who had served alongside him, trusting me enough to share what my dad never would.

Helicopter pilots had the highest casualty rate of any service group in Vietnam—10% of the 57,000-plus who were killed in action were pilots. Over half of the Huey copters my dad flew went down. Every day was a life-or-death situation, but my dad made it through.

"Do you have your dad's yearbook?" Mr. Anderson asked.

I didn't know what he meant, but he explained that military service groups often had yearbooks corresponding to their years in service. About a month after our initial meeting, Mr. Anderson gave me a copy of his yearbook. He trusted me—a stranger he'd met in a parking lot—with one of his most cherished possessions. That's how much he respected my dad.

STEPPING OUT OF YOUR COMFORT ZONE

Amy often reminds me that my life isn't like most people's—that I have a knack for finding "Mr. Andersons" worldwide. She's not wrong. I've met countless people through seemingly random moments, people with whom I've shared incredible commonalities.

But here's the truth: I'm not naturally outgoing. Despite my career as a keynote speaker and software salesman, I'm actually pretty introverted. I like my routines, my privacy, and my downtime. Walking up to a stranger to converse isn't my default mode.

Yet, I do it anyway.

Because sometimes, taking action means stepping out of your comfort zone. It means saying hello when you'd rather stay quiet. It means asking a question when it's easier to keep walking.

That one conversation with Mr. Anderson gave me a deeper connection to my dad than I ever expected. It proved to me that this is a connected world, and those connections are worth pursuing—even if they take effort.

ACTION CREATES CONNECTION

My dad was a hero to me in every sense of the word, but a simple action—getting out of my truck and saying hello—revealed a new layer of his story. It's a lesson I'll never forget.

Loneliness and isolation kill more people than any disease does. That's why it's so important to take action to connect with others. If you see someone wearing something that piques your interest, say something. If you sense a commonality, ask a question. You never know what stories, friendships, or lessons might come from a simple hello.

The world is filled with Mr. Andersons waiting to share their stories. You just have to take the first step.

25

INVEST IN YOURSELF

ACTION

ON THE THREE-HOUR DRIVE to and from Bridgeport to be with me, my mom listened to books on tape. Not music, not the radio—tapes about sales strategies, mindset, and motivation. Tom Hopkins was a regular in the car, teaching sales skills and instilling a positive outlook on life. Being in the car during some of those drives subconsciously helped me realize early on that learning didn't stop at school. People could invest in themselves, even outside of the classroom, to improve their lives. That idea stuck with me.

A TEENAGER AT THE GARDEN

When I was fifteen or sixteen, my mom invited me to see Zig Ziglar speak at Boston Garden. Zig was a legend—polished, quick-witted, and commanding the stage with every line. Even in the twilight of his career, he filled every seat in the Garden. Most of the attendees were professionals—people much older than me. As a teenager, I felt out of place, but I couldn't deny the energy in the room. Hearing stories of resilience, success, and optimism was eye-opening. I left that event feeling inspired, even if I didn't fully understand how to apply what I'd heard.

In my early twenties, I couldn't afford tickets to in-person events, but I caught Tony Robbins on late-night TV. At first, I was skeptical. The big smile, the booming voice—was this guy for real? How could anyone motivate others like this? But years later, his Netflix documentary, I'm Not Your Guru, changed my perspective. Watching him connect with people facing major challenges—and bringing them to laughter, tears, and breakthroughs—it resonated. Not everyone in his audience could have been a "plant." What stuck with me wasn't the grandeur but his ability to make people feel seen and understood.

My first live self-development event came at twenty-nine: the Tom Hopkins Sales Mastery Program in Scottsdale, Arizona. It was a two-to-three-day event with 1,500 attendees, and my team from SD was there too. They tested us on our sales skills, and out of all the participants, I ranked dead last—1,500 out of 1,500.

I could have been embarrassed, but I wasn't. I knew testing wasn't my strength, and honestly, the rankings didn't matter to me. What mattered was applying the lessons I learned to my work and life. I took what I could from the event, and the experience reinforced the importance of growth over perfection.

THE POWER OF CONTINUED LEARNING

Over the years, I've attended dozens of events and programs—live and virtual. Grant Cardone, Patricia Fripp, Chris Daltorio, Tony Robbins, and my personal favorite, Jesse Itzler. Each one left an impression. There's no secret ingredient to success, but the cumulative lessons from these experiences have helped me stay focused and motivated. Self-improvement isn't optional if you want to live your best life—it's essential.

Jesse Itzler's coaching program stands out because of its authenticity. Jesse doesn't push a product or "the next big thing." He shares real habits and hacks, lifting people up without ulterior motives. His live calls brought together 1,500 people from all over the world every month: celebrities, athletes, educators, business leaders, and everyday folks. The advice was valuable—but the human connection was even more impactful.

One of those connections led me to Mark Resnick. Jesse's program brought together people from all walks of life, but the fact that Mark and I lived only twenty minutes apart was pure coincidence. I reached out to him after seeing his name in the program's directory, and that single email set off a chain of events that have changed my life for the better.

THE VALUE OF INVESTING IN YOURSELF

Mark has become one of my closest friends and collaborators. Without him, this book wouldn't exist, and neither would the Be Au Sm movement in its current form. It's not just his shared insights and beliefs that have driven this project forward—it's his willingness to challenge me, hold me accountable, and support me unconditionally. Our shared belief that most of us focus too much on leaving a legacy rather than living one became the cornerstone of this book.

If I hadn't invested in myself—if I hadn't joined Jesse's program—none of this would have happened. That's the real value of self-improvement: It doesn't just change you; it changes the trajectory of your life. The people you meet, the ideas you're exposed to, and the risks you take to grow, those are the moments that shape everything.

When I think back to sitting in the car with my mom listening to sales tapes, or that teenager at Boston Garden feeling out of place, or even the guy who ranked last at a sales conference in Scottsdale, one thing stands out: none of those moments were wasted. Each one was a step forward, however small.

Joining a gym, reading up on your profession, or attending a conference is a great way to invest in yourself. But the real magic happens when you take a chance on learning from others—when you show up, reach out, and open yourself to new possibilities.

Mark's friendship, this book, and the connections I've made through these programs are proof that those small steps can lead to unexpected and transformative outcomes.

Often, the real value of self-improvement is discovering the people and moments that shape the life you want to live.

26

DOING HARD THINGS

ACTION

In 2020, I was half-listening to a Joe Rogan podcast when a guest shared a story that stopped me in my tracks. The guest was Joe De Sena, founder of Spartan Race, talking about how the pandemic had forced the cancellation of more than 300 Spartan events.

At the time, I was grappling with my own COVID-related losses—38 canceled speaking engagements that derailed my year and my finances. I felt devastated. Yet here was Joe, calmly discussing his far bigger setback with unwavering optimism. There wasn't a trace of panic in his words or demeanor. Instead, he radiated resilience and a belief in rebuilding stronger. I couldn't stop listening.

Then he started talking about chickens—specifically, how he picks them up from the post office. That was something I thought only I did! I made a mental note to connect with him down the road but never did.

WHEN ACTION CREATES OPPORTUNITY

Fast forward to May 2024. As I was boarding a flight from Denver to Boston, my phone buzzed with an email notification. It was from Joe De Sena's podcast producer: "Joe is interested in having you on his podcast."

I couldn't believe it. I typed a quick response— "I'm in"—and hit send before boarding. This time, I was determined to make it happen. Being on Joe's podcast would not only amplify the Be Au Sm message to a massive audience but it would also give me a chance to thank him personally. His words on that Rogan episode had helped me get through one of the toughest years of my life.

I dove into research on Joe's incredible journey. From selling t-shirts and running a pool-cleaning business to thriving on Wall Street and eventually founding Spartan Race, his story was a masterclass in grit and action. But I wanted to go beyond research; I wanted to stand out.

That's when I called my friend Chris Mills, owner of Shovel Town Flags, and commissioned a one-of-a-kind Spartan/Be Au Sm wooden flag. The plan was to deliver it personally as a thank-you for his inspiration.

In early July, Joe's producer and I set a date, and in August, I recorded the podcast. I was pumped but also nervous. Joe De Sena is known for pushing people beyond their limits. Would he call me out for being fat and out of shape?

He didn't. Instead, he was kind, encouraging, and focused on lifting me (and others) up. When the podcast wrapped, I presented him with the flag. He was genuinely touched, and to my surprise, he invited me to join his personal heat in the November Spartan Race at Fenway Park.

DOING HARD THINGS

On race day, Saturday, November 9, I woke up early and met my Be Au Sm team outside Fenway Park in the freezing pre-dawn hours. We lined up with the friends-and-family heat, led by Joe himself. As the race began, reality set in—I was nowhere near ready for this. Ninety days of inconsistent training weren't enough, and I felt like quitting multiple times. By the time I reached Obstacle 14, I was toast. Wearing a weighted vest, ducking under cords, and climbing ramps had pushed me to my limits.

Every time I wanted to quit, I'd ask my teammate Bobby Chavez, "You good, Bobby?" Every time he said "yes," I knew I could keep going. We got to the top of one ramp, about halfway through the challenge, and I was ready to throw in the towel. Then I heard a voice from below, not far away, saying, "We do hard things!"

Oh man, here comes Joe. We need to keep going.

We got halfway down, and I was just trying to keep moving. I asked, "*You good, Bobby?*"

Before he could answer, I heard Joe behind us say, "You got this, Bobby!" Joe was now with us. He didn't pass us like so many others had; he stayed right there. We reached the bottom and took off our vests. We were gassed, but Joe didn't leave. He led the way and walked with us.

Joe could have easily encouraged us and kept moving, but he didn't. He saw that we needed extra support and stayed with us for the next twenty minutes. It was one of many examples throughout the morning of Joe leading with G.R.A.C.E. He wanted everyone to win—to realize that we can do extraordinary things—but sometimes, you have to do hard things. It was an incredibly uplifting moment for Bobby and me.

WHO WE BECOME

We can talk all we want about being Au Sm, changing for the better, or overcoming adversity, but words only take us so far. Without action, they're just ideas floating in the air. Action leads to outcomes—not always immediately, but eventually. That is, if we stay the course and put in the work.

It took four years from the moment I first heard Joe De Sena on that podcast to end up running alongside him at Fenway Park. In those years, I faced challenges and doubts. But hearing Joe's voice and his stories of grit and perseverance planted a seed of belief in me. That belief grew into action, and those actions—consistent, small steps—brought me to a place I never thought I'd be: finishing a Spartan Race with a team of people who believed in the same mission.

What stuck with me most wasn't the race itself but the moments in between—the times when Joe stayed back to encourage Bobby and me, reminding us that we could do hard things. It was a lesson I will not forget. Sometimes, action is as simple as showing up for someone else, staying with them when they want to quit, and proving that we can accomplish more than we ever could alone.

What action can you take today to move closer to the person you want to be? What hard thing can you tackle to leave a legacy worth remembering? Because at the end of the day, it's not just about what we achieve—it's about who we become along the way.

CONSISTENCY

SHOWING UP ONCE IS easy. Showing up every day, even when you don't feel like it? That's what sets you apart.

For me, consistency doesn't mean being perfect; it means keeping my word, doing the work, and following through, no matter what. It means honoring commitments, whether to a customer, a friend, or even to myself. It's the reason I kept delivering water to Mrs. Stapleton when it wasn't convenient. It's why I still call three people a week just to check in. It's why I get onstage, write, and speak—not because it's always easy, but because I said I would.

Living your legacy isn't a one-time decision. It's something you do over and over again until it becomes who you are.

27

I GAVE MY WORD

CONSISTENCY

IN THE MID-1990S, MY dad started a spring water delivery company. He purchased the distribution rights for Eastern Massachusetts and a panel van from Providence Airport's Budget Rent-a-Car. Over the next two years, I helped him whenever I could, and after leaving my first sales job in the tech space, I joined the business full-time, delivering five-gallon bottles and coolers to homes and businesses across the region.

GRASSROOTS GROWTH

My dad always stressed the importance of keeping my eyes open for new clients while delivering to existing ones. This meant knocking on the door next to the one I was delivering to and asking our current customers for referrals. Besides a single ad in the Yellow Pages, we had a zero-dollar marketing budget, so we relied on grassroots efforts to grow our business.

This strategy worked well, and over nearly eight years, we built a solid customer base, eventually selling the business to the fourth-largest spring water company in the Northeast in 2003.

One of the most memorable clients I ever had was Mrs. Stapleton. I met her while delivering to a client in Chestnut Hill—a magnificent home where Mrs. Stapleton worked as a longtime caretaker. She was one of the nicest people I've ever met, and although she was pushing eighty, she was full of energy and always present when I made my deliveries.

After about a year of delivering to that home, Mrs. Stapleton asked if I could provide water to her house. She explained that the five-gallon bottles were too heavy for her to handle, so I bought a few three-gallon bottles to see if they would work. But even those were still too heavy for her to lift.

FINDING A SOLUTION

Mrs. Stapleton didn't share much about her personal life, but I sensed that she had experienced some significant losses. Her daughter eventually started getting deliveries, too, which led me to believe Mrs. Singleton's husband had likely passed away before I met her. She was living alone, so everything in her home had to be manageable by herself.

As I was thinking of ways to accommodate Mrs. Stapleton, the bottling plant informed me that they could start providing 16.9-oz bottles in cardboard box cases. It seemed like the perfect solution. I reached out to Mrs. Stapleton with the good news, and she immediately ordered ten cases a month without even asking about the price—just how soon I could deliver.

We scheduled a day and time for the delivery, and she gave me her address. To my surprise, it was nowhere near Chestnut Hill—it was in Mattapan/Dorchester, a neighborhood about 12 miles away where we had no other deliveries. While this didn't fit our plan for growth and route density, I didn't hesitate to tell Mrs. Stapleton I'd be there soon.

On the day of the delivery, I found myself driving through an unfamiliar part of town, sitting at a red light on Blue Hill Avenue or a nearby street. My truck was a Mitsubishi Cab Over, a flat-front vehicle with little horsepower and high torque, and I was driving with the windows down because the air conditioning didn't work. As I waited at the light, I suddenly heard a loud bang and saw someone run in front of my truck.

For a moment, everything seemed surreal. The light turned green, and I started driving again, only to notice that the person who had run by was now lying on the sidewalk. Later, I learned that it had been a gunshot.

As I continued to Mrs. Singleton's house, my mind was racing. "What just happened? Was that really a gunshot? Should I have stopped? Why did I agree to this?" But I kept driving, determined to make my delivery.

MRS. STAPLETON'S STRENGTH

I arrived at Mrs. Stapleton's house on a one-way street near the Franklin Park Zoo. As I pulled up, I noticed a group of five men with a pit bull nearby. They watched me closely as I started unloading the ten cases of water onto my dolly. As they got closer, it became clear they didn't want me there and wanted what I had in the truck.

I was getting more nervous by the second, but then I heard a voice shout, "Hey, leave Josh alone! He's bringing me my water!" It was Mrs. Stapleton, this almost eighty-year-old woman who couldn't lift a three-gallon bottle but was standing up to five tough young men and a pit bull.

One of the men looked up and said, "Okay, Mrs. Stapleton!" With that, the group and the dog walked away, leaving me to finish my delivery.

For years, I didn't share Mrs. Stapleton's story or the gunshot story with anyone. When I finally did, people asked me why I continued to make the delivery. My answer was simple: "Because I said I would be there."

It's easy to make promises but much more challenging to keep them, especially when things don't go as planned. But when you do—when you honor your commitments—you create a reputation for reliability that people come to trust and depend on. Consistency builds trust, not just with others, but within yourself. Following through sets you apart, whether a job, a relationship, or even a simple delivery.

That's what happened with Mrs. Stapleton. I didn't just deliver water; I delivered on a promise. And that consistency, that dedication to doing what I said I would do, made all the difference.

When you stay true to your word, you begin to build a legacy of trust and reliability that others will remember long after the job is done.

28

LEGACY OF LIFTING OTHERS UP

CONSISTENCY

Some people have a natural gift for spotting potential in others. Bill Nixon is one of those people. As the founder and CEO of Willwork, a global company that provides labor for trade show events, Bill built his empire on a single idea, one truck, and a small warehouse in Easton, MA. Today, Willwork employs more than 2,000 people worldwide, but it all started with a simple vision, a relentless work ethic, and a willingness to empower others.

I first met Bill in 1994 when my dad rented warehouse space from him for our spring water business. We started with just under 1,000 square feet for $250 a month. Bill could have easily raised the rent as both his business and ours grew, but he didn't. Instead, he treated the arrangement as more than just a rental agreement—he saw it as a partnership, showing genuine respect for my dad's hard work and character.

Over time, it became clear that Bill was more than just a landlord—he was someone who valued relationships as much as business.

RECOGNIZING POTENTIAL

Apparently, my dad wasn't the only one who impressed Bill. Not long after we moved in, Bill offered me a part-time job helping to set up trade shows in Boston. Bill had an instinct for spotting talent and fostering success. If he saw potential in someone, he'd do whatever it took to help them thrive—whether that meant offering startup money, giving advice, or connecting them to resources. I was lucky enough to be one of those people.

I jumped at the chance. I respected and admired Bill, and I knew this would give me the opportunity to earn a few extra bucks while also getting a front-row seat to how a successful business was run.

For the next ten years, I worked for Bill whenever he needed me, learning from him and observing his leadership up close. He wasn't flashy or overbearing; he led with a quiet confidence that earned the respect of everyone who worked with him. Bill was the kind of person who made you want to do better—not because he demanded it, but because he inspired it.

Some of his guiding principles have stayed with me for life.

These lessons weren't just words. They were the foundation of how Bill built his company and empowered those around him, including me. Here are the top three lessons I learned from Bill:

- Be prompt. Show up on time, ready to work, no exceptions.

- Never say no until you have to. Instead of focusing on what can't be done, Bill taught me to find solutions and lead with what *can* be done.

- Always write a thank-you card. Whether it was for a booth team leader after an event or for a client who trusted us, Bill made sure gratitude was always part of the process.

A LASTING IMPACT

As Willwork grew, Bill's belief in me never wavered. He didn't just teach me how to work hard; he showed me how to value people and invest in their success. Even now, running a $100 million company, he remains grounded. He'll give anyone the time of day if he believes they have something special.

Bill and I have stayed friends over the years, and I still turn to him for advice. No matter how busy he is, he always makes time to listen and offer guidance.

The lessons I learned from Bill extend far beyond the trade show floors. The importance of thank-you cards, for instance. After every event, every t-shirt order, and every speaking engagement, I take the time to write a thank-you note. This isn't just about politeness—you are acknowledging the value of people's time, trust, and support.

Empowering others doesn't always mean giving advice or offering opportunities—it's about showing up, seeing people for who they are, and investing in their growth. Bill Nixon's example reminds me to do the same for others—to look for potential, provide support, and celebrate their successes.

Empowerment is a two-way street. You should recognize the people who lift you up and make sure you do the same for others. Bill empowered me not just through words but through his actions. He saw something in me and gave me opportunities to succeed.

Who in your life can you empower today? Maybe the better question is: who in your life could use a kind word, a moment of encouragement, or simply someone to listen without judgement?

Take a page from Bill Nixon's playbook: Invest in people, lead with gratitude, and always believe in the power of what *can be done*—because done consistently, that's how you build a legacy that truly lasts.

29

DO YOUR HOMEWORK

CONSISTENCY

GROWING UP, THERE WAS something I didn't take seriously enough—homework. But today, I approach it with intensity, and that mindset extends to everything I do, especially when it comes to preparation and showing up for others.

In 2023, I was asked to speak to the Norwalk, CT, Varsity Basketball team about togetherness and teamwork. I could have easily shared my experiences working with companies like Willwork Global Event Services, Hanes Group, Berkshire Mountain Spring Water, Purview, K12 Pros, and OperationsHERO. I could have talked about how working together and leading without a title helped us become market leaders and make a difference in our clients' lives.

But instead, I chose to do my homework.

GOING THE EXTRA MILE

I researched the program online and discovered an inspiring story about Jaylen Brown, a 5'9" senior who had just scored his second fifty-point game of the season—and he didn't even start playing basketball until his sophomore year. That kind of story speaks volumes about *dedication* and *perseverance*.

I also drove down early and quietly observed their practice without the team knowing why I was there. I wanted to see the team dynamics firsthand and understand the players' energy and roles.

During my talk, I didn't just focus on the star players; I recognized the importance of every team member. I presented one team member, Charlie, with a Be Au Sm T-shirt for being his team's biggest supporter and cheerleader. Anytime there was clapping or words of encouragement, Charlie was leading the way. He may not have been the one scoring points, but he was as critical to the team's success as anyone else.

SETTING AN EXAMPLE

Young people look to adults in their lives more than we realize. Even when they don't say it outright, they're watching how we show up—our preparation, our effort, our attitude. We may never know the full extent of our impact, but it's there.

When we take shortcuts or rely on past successes, we send the wrong message. But when we put in the extra effort—doing our homework, showing up early, and recognizing each person's value—we set an example of what leadership and commitment look like.

These high school athletes didn't need a motivational talk—they needed to see someone who cared enough to understand their story and celebrate their unique contributions.

CONSISTENCY IN HOW YOU SHOW UP

Consistency is about how you show up. Put in the effort, demonstrate that you care, and go the extra mile. Whether speaking to a group of high school athletes or working with a client, the preparation you put in beforehand makes all the difference.

Young people are the future, and they need role models who show them what's possible. They need to see adults who embody the values of hard work, preparation, and care. Consistency is the key to unlocking your full potential and making a real difference in the lives of others. It's not just about success in business or sports—it's about living your legacy with purpose and intention.

The next time you're called upon to step up, ask yourself: *Have I done my homework? Am I going to bring my best effort?*

Because someone is always watching—and your example could be the spark that lights their path.

30

2,487 DAYS

CONSISTENCY

TRAVEL MEANS DIFFERENT THINGS to different people. For some, it's an exciting escape or a chance to explore new places. For others, it's simply part of the daily grind, especially when it comes to business travel. No matter what kind of traveler you are, we get used to things running smoothly. And when they don't, it's easy to feel frustrated, stressed, or downright angry.

As someone who spends a lot of time in airports and on planes, I've learned to appreciate how much can actually go right when traveling. In the last seven years of constant flying, I hadn't experienced a major hiccup in 2,487 days. That's a LONG time to go without an unplanned overnight stay due to a missed connection or canceled flight.

When a disruption finally happened, I could've easily let the frustration take over. But instead, I chose to focus on the positive—that this was a rare disruption after years of smooth travel. A week later, it happened again—another canceled flight, another unexpected overnight stay. But this time, I hadn't checked my luggage yet, so I had clean clothes and toiletries. Funny how little things can make a huge difference when things don't go as planned.

Looking back at 2023, I visited thirty-four states and one Canadian province, took over a hundred flights, and drove thousands of miles in rental cars. I was honored to speak with over 100,000 people at over one hundred events. It was a whirlwind year. I'm grateful to everyone who has shared their belief in me, whether for a Be Au Sm speaking opportunity, an OperationsHERO client, or a K12 Pros professional development contract. These moments of connection keep me going, even when the travel gets tough.

INTENTIONAL CHOICES

Despite occasional delays and unexpected overnights, I've learned that keeping a positive attitude helps me handle whatever comes next. It's not always easy, and I'm certainly not perfect. I still get frustrated, but I remind myself that keeping a steady approach helps me bounce back faster.

Lately, I've been trying meditation. I'm not doing it every day yet (still working on that consistency!), but I've noticed a difference. I feel more present with my family, calmer under duress, and less bothered by things out of my control, like delayed flights, traffic, or long lines at my favorite Honey Dew coffee shop.

Living with G.R.A.C.E. is more than a concept; it's a daily practice. It's waking up every day and deciding to choose gratitude, resilience, action, consistency, and empowerment—even when life doesn't make it easy. You can't wait for things to magically align or to have everything go right; you need to find meaning and momentum in the moments that test you most.

That's where growth happens—one intentional choice at a time.

31

REACH OUT AND CALL SOMEONE

CONSISTENCY

FOR OVER TEN YEARS, I've made it a habit to call three random people from my contacts each week. There's no agenda, no specific reason for the calls—just a genuine check-in to see how they're doing. It's not flashy, but it's one of the most meaningful things I do.

Why do I do it? Because communicating on social media or through a quick text isn't the same as truly connecting. Sure, texting three people a week would be faster and more convenient. But it's not as genuine. Picking up the phone and making a call shows you care. It takes effort. And that effort matters.

I can't tell you how many times I've heard "You made my day" or "You don't know how much I appreciate this call." It's not really about me. It's the fact that someone took the time to call. A simple phone call can turn someone's day around, and in many cases, I've learned things I never would have known otherwise: that someone is dealing with an illness, navigating an aging parent's care, or supporting a sick child. These things don't typically come up in a quick text exchange or a comment on social media.

But what most people don't realize is that these calls have made my day more times than I can count, too. I'm glued to my phone all day long, but the truth is, my phone doesn't ring very often. There's something deeply rewarding about hearing someone's voice, sharing a laugh, or just being there to listen when they need it most.

I've had people admit that my call came at the lowest point of their lives. And while I didn't know it then, the simple act of picking up the phone made a difference for them and me.

Just three calls a week, 52 weeks a year—156 calls annually. This small, consistent action has become a cornerstone of how I connect with others. I scroll through my contacts, choose people I haven't spoken to in a while, and reach out.

CONSISTENCY: THE ESSENTIAL ELEMENT

Consistency isn't always easy. Life is busy, routines get disrupted, and it's easy to let even the best intentions slide. Have you ever attended a workshop or conference and learned something game-changing, only to let it fade over time? I've been there. We all have.

But this practice has stuck with me because I've seen its impact—not just on the people I call but on myself. It's a reminder that small, consistent actions can create big results over time.

Consistency is the thread that weaves the fabric of living your legacy. Each element is essential—but without consistency, the others unravel. You don't have to be exceptional every single time. Rather, create a steady rhythm of commitment, a constant decision to act even when the results aren't immediate or guaranteed.

When I think back on these calls, it's not the words exchanged that matter most—it's the pattern of care they represent. Week after week, year after year, they've become a quiet testament to what's possible when you commit to a practice. A legacy is shaped by the habits you choose to sustain and the values you choose to live, one consistent action at a time.

What's one thing you can do, not just once, but over and over, that aligns with the life you want to live and the legacy you want to leave? Commit to it. Let that action speak louder than your intentions, louder than your doubts. Because in the end, it's not what we do occasionally that defines us; it's what we commit to consistently that leaves a mark.

32

POLISHING SHOES & SMILES

CONSISTENCY

SALES IS OFTEN DESCRIBED as the art of identifying a person's pain or need and then providing a solution. But sometimes, the most meaningful solutions don't address a need—they spark a connection.

One morning, as I rushed through Terminal A at Kansas City International Airport, shineologist Angela M. stopped me in my tracks with a simple observation.

"Your sneakers could use a shine!"

With all the delays and chaos that come with air travel, I hadn't even noticed that my "speaker sneakers" were scuffed and dull from salt, sand, and snow. Angela was right—they were a mess.

As Angela got to work, I had the chance to chat with her and learn about her remarkable journey. She's been shining shoes for over twenty-five years, but her real shine isn't just in the polish—it's in her smile, her energy, and the way she genuinely connects with her customers.

THE POWER OF CONSISTENCY

Angela isn't just good at her job—she's passionate about it. Day after day, she shows up with the same enthusiasm, kindness, and attention to detail that makes every customer feel special. In a world where so many people are just "getting through the day," Angela is a rare example of someone who brings her whole self to her work. *Every. Single. Time.*

It struck me how rare—and powerful—that kind of consistency is. Angela's pride in her work and her ability to connect with people is a testament to the power of small, consistent acts done with heart.

After Angela finished shining my sneakers, we decided to take a picture together. The first person we asked accidentally cut off my hat, but instead of letting it ruin the moment, we laughed and asked someone else. It's a small memory, but one that sticks with me—just like Angela's unwavering positivity.

THE SHINE OF CONSISTENCY

Angela doesn't just polish shoes—she polishes the lives of everyone she meets, one smile at a time. By stopping, connecting, and appreciating the people around us, we open ourselves to the positive energy they bring. Whether through a friendly conversation, a smile, or a well-timed shoeshine, these moments of gratitude help us see the good in our everyday lives.

You don't have to polish shoes like Angela to understand that work is about showing up for others with energy and care, no matter what's going on in our personal lives. Consistency is about being present. It's about doing the little things well, again and again, until they become a part of who you are.

If you're ever in Terminal A, take a moment to walk by Angela's stand. She'll tell you if your shoes need a shine and do it with a smile. It's not just her service that will impress; it's the connection and care she brings to her work.

Thank you, Angela, for reminding me to appreciate the small things and bringing a little extra shine to my day.

33

BUILD A LEGACY OF SUPPORT

CONSISTENCY

TERRY AND TODD HEDRICK are twins. We met in the third grade and have been friends ever since. They are my oldest friends, and we've been there for each other from the beginning.

Unlike me, these guys were athletes, which opened them up to a whole new group of friends. Still, the Hedrick twins stayed with me. In high school, I drove them to school each day. On weekends, I was such a fixture at their house that Mr. Hedrick said he was going to declare me a dependent for tax purposes.

Even after the FBI raided my home and arrested my dad, Terry and Todd stuck by me. I was proud to be with them at their weddings and honored and humbled to be asked to give the eulogy at their older brother Tim's funeral mass.

You probably have friends like this in your life—one or two, maybe more if you're lucky. The older we get, the more cherished these friends become. That kind of consistency is hard to find, but when you do, it's priceless.

THE STEADY ANCHOR OF COLLEAGUES *AND* CRITICS

In my professional life, I've also been blessed to be friends with people who are the epitome of consistency. The first is Pat Buchanan. He's the smartest person I know. He, Scott Carpenter, and I have been working together for the past twenty-seven years. From 2004 to 2009, while working for SD, every time I visited North Carolina, I slept on Pat's couch. I doubt we've had more than four arguments the entire time we've known each other.

Andy Townshend is another person I have worked with for a long time. He's the Texas rep for OperationsHERO and is super successful. Unlike me, Andy is polished, organized, and methodical. Different styles but the same results. What makes our relationship work so well despite our differences is our genuine take on life: Consistency is the key—be yourself and care about the work you do.

It amazes me how many sales professionals seem not to care about their work. For them, it's just a paycheck, and some will do anything to get a sale. In fact, my total disgust with many sales professionals is what prompted me almost nine years ago to want to write a book in the first place.

Colleagues are one thing, but what about customers? I am not afraid to admit that my personality isn't fit for everyone. Charley Braham from Missouri is now a close friend (and customer) of mine, but it's no secret he despised me upon our first meeting.

Often, I am loud and direct—sometimes offensive—but not in a malicious way. But once he figured out that I was genuine, generous, and deeply passionate about what I do for a living, he embraced me. Not because I changed who I was to fit Charley's preferences, but because I stayed true to who I am.

I'm grateful, too, because Charley is one of the hardest-working, most consistent individuals I know. Every phone call or meeting we share is a learning experience, and I value his thoughts and friendship tremendously.

THE POWER OF CONSISTENCY

One way to live your legacy is to emulate the best traits of those you interact with—at the office, on the road, out to dinner, or in your hometown. Consistency is the glue that holds it all together.

If you want to be the best version of yourself—if you want to live your legacy—you need to embrace the element of consistency. The friends, colleagues, and customers who remain by your side do so because they value your authenticity.

Being consistent in who you are—not who others want you to be—is one of the greatest gifts you can give to yourself and the people in your life.

EMPOWERMENT

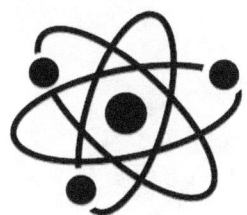

No one does it alone.

Every success, every breakthrough, every moment that changed my life for the better happened because someone believed in me—often before I believed in myself.

When you're empowered, you don't wait for permission. Instead, you recognize your strength and use it to make other people better. You show up for people in ways that remind them what they're capable of. Empowerment is a small encouragement at the right time, a push to take that next step, or simply believing in someone when they don't yet have that confidence in themselves.

For me, empowerment has come in all forms—through a conversation with a flight attendant, a challenge from a mentor, a friend who refused to let me quit, or even a reminder from my own son that when you think positive thoughts, good things happen.

34

A LIFE OF PURPOSE

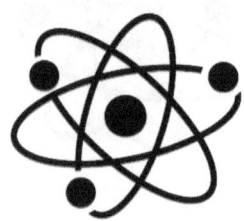

EMPOWERMENT

I WAS MEETING WITH a customer in 2023 when I heard a story that immediately caught my attention. He told me about a team member named Clyde, who arrives to work an hour early every day, turns in his unused vacation days, and has no plans to retire. My response was simple: I need to meet Clyde before today ends.

During lunch, I did just that—and it turned out to be one of the most Au Sm experiences of my professional career.

THE LEGEND OF CLYDE

Clyde grew up in a farming family, served his country as a veteran, and has loved every single day of work for the past seventeen years at his current job. Sharp as a tack, Clyde is one of the most skilled equipment operators I've ever seen, and his entire team holds him in the highest regard.

But what really floored me was when Clyde shared his thoughts on retirement. While he's technically just fifteen years away from collecting a full pension, he told me, "I think I have twenty good years of work left before I retire."

Oh, and did I mention that Clyde is ninety-two years old?

Clyde isn't working for a paycheck—he's working because he loves what he does. He's not counting down the days to retirement—he's counting the days he still gets to contribute.

Clyde's story is a masterclass in empowerment. No one—not a calendar, not society, not anyone—gets to decide when it's time to stop doing what fulfills you. If you love what you do, and you still have the drive, keep going.

When Clyde said, "I think I have twenty good years of work left," it wasn't a boast—it was a statement of how much he values his work and the life he's created through it.

PASSION FUELS EMPOWERMENT

Clyde reminded me of something simple yet powerful: When you find meaning in what you do, you bring your best self to it every single day.

That's empowerment. It's not about working forever—it's about working with purpose. Whether you're 22 or 92, when you do something that fuels you, it doesn't just empower you—it empowers those around you. Clyde's presence, energy, and commitment uplift everyone on his team.

So whatever it is you love—your career, your craft, your mission—lean into it. Find joy in it. Keep driving. Because when you own your purpose, age doesn't limit you—it empowers you.

35

ONE SECOND OF HOPE

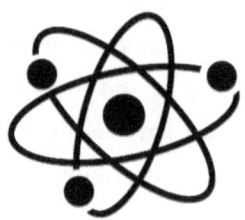

EMPOWERMENT

"I LOVE THE SHIRT—BE Au Sm!"

It was my last flight of 2021, and I was emotionally drained. After an unplanned fifteen-month hiatus from speaking due to COVID, I was back on the road. But it wasn't the travel that had left me feeling wiped—it was the uncertainty. Be Au Sm was my dream, but I wasn't sure it was going to make it as a company.

The flight attendant's comment made me smile, and we struck up a conversation. We talked about holiday travel, the stress of the season, and the chaos in the terminal. She must have seen the exhaustion on my face because her calm, easy energy started to lift my spirits. It wasn't just her words—it was her presence. For the first time in weeks, I felt a glimmer of optimism.

THE POWER OF ONE SECOND

That optimism didn't last long. Once we were in the air, I found myself spiraling back into doubt. Usually, I spend flights preparing for keynotes or catching up on work, but on this one, I couldn't focus. My mind kept circling back to my future and whether I had what it took to make Be Au Sm a success.

As we began our descent into Boston, the flight attendant's voice came over the intercom. She did the usual "Welcome to Boston" routine, but then she added something extra.

"Not everyone on this plane needs to hear this, but there is at least one person who does. We can live forty days without food, three days without water, eight minutes without air . . . but only one second without hope."

Her words hit me hard. In that moment, I realized how much I'd let fear and doubt cloud my ability to move forward.

WHEN HOPE FEELS OUT OF REACH

That wasn't the first time I needed to be reminded of the power of hope—and it certainly won't be the last. When I lost my job with SD, I was hopeless in the truest sense. Those first hours, sitting in my office and wondering what was next, were some of the darkest of my life.

It was Les Trachtman and Ed Roshitsh who pulled me out of that pit. Their check-ins weren't just check-ins—they lifted me up and helped me believe in myself again. Their faith in me reignited something inside that I thought had burned out.

"Hope is not a strategy" is a phrase often used in military planning and business leadership—and for good reason. You can't rely solely on hope to solve problems or achieve success. Hope without action is just a wish.

But that doesn't mean hope is unimportant. Hope paired with action becomes a force of change. A plan gives hope direction, and small steps forward—even imperfect ones—can turn hope into empowerment.

Believing in yourself is the cornerstone of empowerment, but sometimes, we all need a nudge to get there. When we're stuck and not feeling Au Sm, two things need to happen: We need to find hope, and we need to act.

Sometimes, hope comes from the simplest places—a random conversation, a kind word, or even a reminder over an airplane intercom. That flight attendant didn't know my story or how much her words would resonate, but they did. And here's the best part about hope—it's contagious. When we give hope to others, we remind them that they matter. A text, a call, a quick conversation—that's all it takes to empower someone who might be struggling.

LIVING WITH EMPOWERMENT

Hope alone won't get us through difficult patches in life, but it's a vital spark that keeps us moving forward. Pair it with action, and you can overcome anything. That flight and that moment reminded me that even someone who empowers others for a living needs to be empowered in return.

We all have the power to offer hope to someone else. And sometimes, that hope comes back to us in unexpected ways, giving us exactly what we need to keep going.

Hope doesn't stop, and it doesn't fail. It just needs a second to be heard—and someone willing to take action to keep it alive.

36

CLAIM YOUR SUPERPOWER

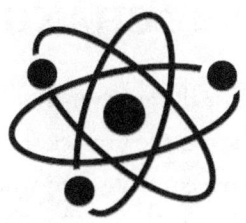

EMPOWERMENT

I'VE NEVER BEEN CLINICALLY diagnosed with ADHD, but trust me, I know I have it. And honestly, I see it as one of my superpowers.

That's not to say it doesn't come with challenges. My brain is always running, making it hard to relax or shut things off. Sleep doesn't come easily, and convincing myself I don't need much has become more of a coping mechanism than a truth.

Another hallmark of ADHD? Getting things to the one-yard line—but never quite scoring the touchdown. How many of you can relate? You start projects with a fire inside you, but somewhere along the way, the spark dims. The follow-through just isn't there.

For a long time, I kept my struggles locked away. I never talked about feeling abandoned by two father figures or what it was like growing up with grandparents who barely spoke English. I bottled up grief over losing my friend. Even being fired from SD—a defining moment in my life—was something I kept to myself.

I blamed myself for everything. And when that didn't feel right, I blamed others. Regret piled on regret, and I felt like I was drowning in my own thoughts.

I didn't seek therapy to control my ADHD, but it turned out to be the game-changer I didn't know I needed.

THERAPY: A GAME CHANGER

Seeing a therapist was the last thing I ever thought I'd do, but it changed my life. Therapy gave me the tools to unpack those bottled-up feelings and recognize what was within my control—and what wasn't.

The biggest lesson I learned? You can't control everything, but you can control your mindset. That doesn't mean every day will be Au Sm. Some days will flat-out suck. But therapy doesn't teach you to strive for perfection. Instead, it gives you the skills to wake up with intention and approach each day with the mindset of living your legacy.

Be Au Sm wasn't launched to control what happens in life. It's about how we approach it. We must learn to accept that not everything that happens to us is our fault—and that we have the responsibility, and the power, to respond with resilience, positivity, and action.

Claiming your superpower is part of that journey. Yes, you have super-powers. We all do. They might not feel "super," but they're uniquely yours. Maybe you're great at problem-solving, calming others, or staying focused under pressure.

Take a moment to name them. If you're stuck, try these exercises below. You'll see how they are more like mirrors, reflecting your strengths, values, and the impact you've already made.

- Write a list of things you're grateful for.

- Reflect on the people who inspire you.

- Recall moments when you stepped up, big or small.

THE POWER OF LETTING GO

Letting go isn't easy for me. I've held on to regrets, grudges, and guilt far longer than I should have. But empowerment isn't just about pushing forward—it's also about releasing what weighs you down.

That doesn't mean forgiving every person who has wronged you or pretending certain moments didn't hurt. But forgiveness frees you. It gives you the space to focus on what you can control.

When you stop wasting energy on things outside your influence—traffic, rude people, canceled flights, other people's opinions—you free yourself to focus on what truly matters. Empowerment is about redirecting your energy to what you can influence: your actions, your mindset, and how you use your unique gifts to make a difference.

EMPOWERMENT STARTS WITH YOU

Therapy helped me release what weighed me down. Claiming my superpowers reminded me what I was capable of. And choosing to focus on what I can control gave me the freedom to live with G.R.A.C.E.

Here's what I now know to be true—empowerment isn't just about you. The more you own your strengths, the more you empower others to do the same. When you embrace what makes you unique, when you stop holding onto what doesn't serve you, and when you decide to lead with purpose—you inspire others to do the same.

Empowerment isn't something we wait for. It's something we claim. That's how you live your legacy—and that's what it means to Be Au Sm.

37

PRODUCING GREAT RESULTS

EMPOWERMENT

IN THE EARLY 1990S, my friend Adam moved to Cape Cod with a big dream: to start a produce delivery company. His plan was simple—buy fresh produce in Boston and deliver it to restaurants on the Cape. He bought a van, hit the road, and hustled to build his business. On weekends, I'd ride along and spend hours talking about life, work, and his vision for the company.

One day, Adam shared a concern with me. A big competitor in Boston had slashed their lettuce prices by 30%, and he wasn't sure what to do.

"Should I lower my prices to match theirs?" he asked, visibly worried.

Without hesitation, I said, "Absolutely not. Your company's name is Guaranteed Fresh—not Guaranteed Cheapest. Don't compete on price when you're offering a better service. Focus on what makes you different."

It felt like a passing conversation at the time, but fast-forward a few decades—Adam and I crossed paths again. He had just sold his business after years of incredible success.

During our conversation, he thanked me.

"For what?" I asked, genuinely surprised.

"That advice you gave me back in the '90s," he said. "Not lowering my prices and focusing on quality shaped my entire business strategy. It made all the difference."

I was floored. A few words I barely remembered saying had influenced Adam's entire career. It was a powerful reminder that sometimes, the smallest conversations can leave the biggest mark.

BELIEVING IN OTHERS

In 2021, I met Vai, a young man from India working in customer service at a health tech company. He had moved to Boston for his master's degree and was still adjusting to life in a new country. Our interactions were brief at first, but one day, his supervisor called me and said, "Can you check in on Vai? He's having a rough time."

When I called, Vai explained that several customers had asked to speak to someone else because they couldn't understand his accent. Each rejection chipped away at his confidence, and he was starting to feel defeated.

"Vai," I said, "the next time a customer does that, give them this number." I rattled off my home phone number. "Tell them to call me, and I'll take care of it."

There was a long pause on the other end of the line. "Are you serious?" he asked, sounding both skeptical and relieved.

"Completely serious," I said. "And remember this: You've got this. You're capable, smart, and the right person for this job. Don't let anyone make you feel otherwise."

I never got a call from any of Vai's customers, but something shifted. His confidence soared, and it showed in how he carried himself at work. That small gesture—a phone number and a few encouraging words—empowered Vai to believe in himself again.

THE RESPONSIBILITY OF EMPOWERMENT

What struck me in both stories is how empowerment often happens in the simplest moments. It doesn't take a title, a program, or a grand stage. It happens in car rides, in casual conversations, in a phone call when someone is struggling.

Empowerment is about seeing potential in someone else, even when they don't see it in themselves. Adam didn't realize his strength was in offering quality over quantity. Vai didn't know he had the resilience to thrive in a challenging environment. Sometimes, all it takes is a little belief from someone else to help unlock that potential.

But here's the other side of that coin—our words can do the opposite, too. We can tear someone down in an instant. A sarcastic remark, a dismissive comment, or an unintentional brush-off can leave lasting doubt in someone's mind. That's why how we respond matters.

EMPOWER INTENTIONALLY

The next time someone comes to you with a dream, an idea, or even a doubt—pause before responding. Ask yourself: Am I truly listening? Am I offering thoughtful feedback? Am I leaving them better off than when the conversation began?

Empowerment isn't about handing out compliments or agreeing with every idea. True empowerment is about challenging people to be their best while making sure they know they are capable, valued, and supported.

I didn't know that a conversation in a delivery van in the '90s would change Adam's future. I didn't expect that offering my phone number to

Vai would shift his confidence. But that's the beauty of it—we never really know how much our words and actions mean to someone else.

Empowerment starts with belief—the belief that your words carry weight, that your encouragement matters, and that you have the power to help someone see what they can't yet see in themselves.

That's not just empowerment. That's living your legacy.

38

JUST KEEP PADDLING

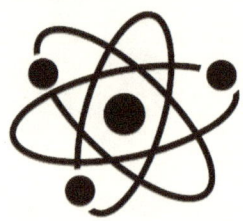

EMPOWERMENT

In 2014, my son Danny was in the first grade. His school was participating in a statewide competition to grow a giant pumpkin, and they needed a $1,200 scale to weigh the pumpkins. To fund the scale, the school created a GoFundMe page, but weeks went by without a single donation.

That's when I told Amy, "Have the coordinator meet me at the pumpkin patch. Let's figure this out."

On the day of the meeting, a Subaru pulled into the lot, and out stepped a face I hadn't seen in decades: Todd Sandstrum, my childhood adversary from pond hockey days.

"Holy shit, Todd Sandstrum, what are you doing here?" I asked, genuinely shocked.

"Holy shit, Josh Peach, what are you doing here?" he fired back with equal surprise.

"I'm here to meet the pumpkin guy," I said.

"I am the pumpkin guy," Todd replied.

What began as a funny and unexpected reunion turned into something far more meaningful. We spent twenty minutes catching up, and by the end of the conversation, I'd committed to the full $1,200 for the scale. I didn't know how or why, but I knew it was the right thing to do.

BUILDING BRIDGES AND PUMPKINS

The pumpkins were planted, the scale was bought, and Todd and I rekindled our friendship. Years of childhood animosity were laid to rest, and we found common ground, including a shared mission to teach kids about where their food comes from and encourage sustainable practices.

We didn't win the pumpkin-growing competition, but that wasn't the point. The real victory was in supporting Danny's school and reconnecting with Todd.

A few months later, Todd called with a new idea. "We're doing the pumpkin contest again next year," he said. "But I've got something even bigger planned. I'm submitting a proposal to the Guinness Book of World Records to paddle the longest distance in a carved pumpkin. You in?"

"Hell yes," I said without hesitation.

Guinness approved his proposal, and two farms donated 800-pound pumpkins. We carved cockpits into the pumpkins and charted a course down a local river.

In September 2015, Todd and I hit the water, aiming to paddle 3.5 miles. Sitting on our knees in the carved-out pumpkins was uncomfortable, to say the least. I only made it two miles before my pumpkin sank. Todd completed the course, but Guinness couldn't award us the record because we didn't properly document the event.

Not to be deterred, we tried again the following year. This time, the goal was 9 miles, paddling from the Taunton Yacht Club to Battleship Cove in Fall River.

PADDLING THROUGH ADVERSITY

About 2.5 miles in, I was ready to quit. My legs were numb, and I felt like I couldn't go on. My friend, Kenny Wertz, paddling beside me in a canoe, was my only source of support. Kenny is one of those rare people who shows up, no matter what. He doesn't ask for recognition or fanfare; he just gives. That day, he gave me his presence and encouragement.

"I can't feel my legs," I told him. "I'm done."

Before I could climb out of the pumpkin, I remembered that I had promised to call Aron Ralston while on the water. Aron is the guy who, after becoming pinned by a boulder in a Utah canyon, cut off his arm to survive.

"Peach, you did it!" Aron exclaimed when I called.

"Not really," I replied. "I've only gone two and a half miles."

"I thought you were doing nine miles?" he asked.

"I can't feel my legs," I admitted.

"You don't need your legs," was his only response before hanging up.

His words hit me hard. Here was a man who had survived one of the most extreme experiences imaginable, and I was complaining about numb legs in a giant pumpkin.

I got back in the water and paddled the remaining miles, finishing in six hours and twenty-two minutes. Todd completed the course in five hours. Though we didn't set the Guinness record (someone had already paddled 45.6 miles in a pumpkin), the experience was life changing.

WHO CAN YOU EMPOWER?

Empowerment often comes in moments we least expect—like a river, a pumpkin, and a call from someone who knows what true adversity looks like. That day on the water, I was struggling. I was ready to quit. But Todd had the vision to chase something bigger. Kenny showed up with steady encouragement. And Aron, with just a few words, reminded me that my biggest obstacle wasn't my legs—it was my mindset.

We all need people like that in our lives. The ones who show up, push us forward, and remind us of our own strength when we've forgotten it. But empowerment isn't something we just receive—it's something we give.

Kenny had my back when I needed it most, just like I've had the backs of others in their own moments of doubt. Aron's words pushed me forward, just like a simple conversation or small gesture can push someone else forward. Empowerment isn't about waiting for the right moment to lift someone up—it's about choosing to do it whenever we can, in big ways or small.

So who in your life needs that extra nudge? Who needs a reminder that they're capable of more than they think?

Because if we've learned anything from this crazy journey—whether it's paddling a pumpkin down a river or pushing through life's harder moments—it's that none of us get through it alone. We all need encouragement. We all need someone in our corner. And we all have the power to be that person for someone else.

39

THE POWER OF A PERSONAL TOUCH

EMPOWERMENT

In August 2007, we bought my parents' house. If you've never purchased a home before, let me warn you:your mailbox will suddenly be bombarded with offers—insurance companies, landscapers, alarm system installers, window repair specialists—you name it, they'll send you a flyer. Most of these get tossed without a second glance, but one small handwritten note caught my eye.

It was a 3" x 5" postcard with a simple message:

"I clean your house. Here is my phone number. References available."

No name. No branding. Just effort.

"We're going to hire this person," I told Amy.

"Why?" she asked, looking at the plain card.

"Because this person went above and beyond," I said. "They scanned the real estate listings, wrote out this card by hand, and delivered it themselves. That's someone who's putting in the work and deserves an opportunity."

A few days later, two women showed up. One didn't speak a word of English, but their native tongue was Portuguese—my grandmother's language. Thanks to my grandmother's interpreting, we hired them on the spot.

THE JOURNEY OF EMPOWERMENT

One of the women was Josie, and she became our regular cleaner. When we hired her, she didn't speak any English, but that didn't stop her from doing her work with precision and care. Over time, her efforts paid off—not just in how she cleaned our home, but in how she built her business.

"You were my first customer," she told Amy the last time she came to the house. "I didn't speak any English when you hired me, but now I do. You gave me so many new customers and helped me grow my business."

Josie stayed with us for five years before returning to Brazil to help run her family's business. She left with a full heart and a thriving career, and I couldn't have been prouder to know that we had played a small role in her success.

It reminded me of my own experience years ago when I worked at the cell phone store, specifically, the day I stayed late to help Bob Bogardus (Chapter 17, Getting Fired). I didn't have to stay, but I wanted to, and because I did, Bob offered me a job on the spot. That encounter will always stick with me because it shows how the smallest acts of service and kindness can have lasting impacts.

RECOGNIZING POTENTIAL

What stood out to me about Josie wasn't a polished brochure or an impressive résumé. It was her initiative. She saw an opportunity, acted on it with nothing more than a handwritten note, and followed through with hard work and determination.

Empowering others doesn't require monumental action. It does require noticing when someone has gone the extra mile and responding with trust and opportunity.

The world is filled with Josies—hardworking, kind, and trustworthy people who just need someone to believe in them. Every time we take the time to support someone, whether by giving a chance or offering encouragement, we plant a seed. When nurtured, that seed can grow into something extraordinary.

Josie's handwritten note led to five years of trust, support, and mutual growth. And my small gesture of staying late for Bob changed the trajectory of my career. Empowerment doesn't always announce itself with big fanfare. Often, it starts with small moments of connection and support.

Ask yourself, how often do you go out of your way for someone? Make it a habit, and you'll empower more people than you can imagine. And just like Josie and Bob, the impact of those moments may return to you in ways you never expected.

40

ONE TO TWENTY YEARS

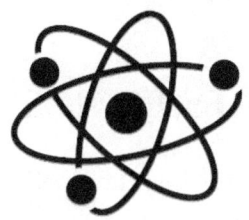

EMPOWERMENT

I MET RON McCULLEY in February 2005. He was the director of purchasing for a school district in Colorado, and we connected immediately. One night, I took him to dinner in Boston's North End. It wasn't just an ordinary table—we were in the restaurant's basement, tucked away in the wine cellar, surrounded by the aromas and ambiance of fine wine. That's when I discovered we were both fans of Tuaca, an Italian liquor.

Though Ron is twenty years older than I am, he's a big kid at heart, and we became close friends. Every year, he puts together a Christmas CD called Rockin' Ronnie's Holiday Hits and sends it to his friends. He's constantly doing thoughtful things for others and has this unique way of bringing people together. Ron is a rare person who exudes positivity, and being around him always leaves you feeling lighter.

In November 2010, Ron was diagnosed with cancer. He needed stem cell treatment, and I learned about it during a Red Sox vs. Cubs game.

It was a unique game—a once-in-a-century matchup between the two teams—and I remember thinking it was one of those nights destined to be a great memory.

Upon hearing Ron's news, a colleague bluntly asked him, "So, how long do you have?"

Ron, true to form, didn't miss a beat. "Well, they told me anywhere from one to twenty years," he replied. "And I plan on taking the liberal side of that number—so twenty years."

His sense of humor and determination were, and still are, unshakable.

LIVING WITH RESILIENCE

I've faced some near-death experiences myself, but living with a terminal illness is an entirely different kind of mental toughness. Ron has lived with this diagnosis for over fifteen years now, and he's still full of life, love, and energy. He's just a miraculous inspiration.

Ron's journey and his unwavering attitude in the face of his diagnosis have profoundly empowered me. Seeing him live joyfully and intentionally despite uncertainty has reminded me that empowerment isn't about control but resilience, choice, and perspective.

Ron's example hast taught me that no matter the challenge, you can choose to find humor, create connections, and lift others up. I don't look at Ron as a cancer victim. I see him as Ron, one of my life's most special people, and if he can handle rough times, then so can I.

Thanks to Ron, I know empowerment is about living fully, right here and now, and that's a lesson I carry with me. He lives as if each day is a gift—not by ignoring his diagnosis, but by rising above it. Through his humor, generosity, and unstoppable spirit, he's shown me that empowerment comes from facing some of life's hardest challenges with courage and an open heart.

41

WHEN "IF" BECOMES "WHEN"

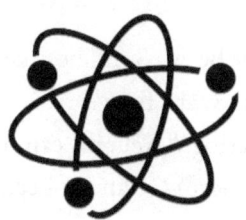

EMPOWERMENT

In EARLY 2020, I had thirty-nine keynotes booked and felt like Be Au Sm was finally turning into my full-time career. I was in North Carolina for a SD conference, listening to a keynote speaker with an incredible story. Yet, despite her amazing story, her delivery felt flat. She was earning $25,000 per keynote, while I was earning $5,000. That moment was eye-opening—I knew I had the potential to make this work as a full-time business.

But just as quickly as the dream began to take shape, everything changed.

COVID-19 exploded onto the scene in March 2020. On March 13, the world shut down, and within 96 hours, 38 out of my 39 keynotes were canceled. What I had worked so hard to build seemed to unravel overnight. My dream of turning Be Au Sm into a full-time career came to a screeching halt.

That year was one of the toughest I've faced. Like so many others, I found myself scrambling to adapt, rebuilding my speaking business bit by bit. But even as I made progress, doubts lingered. Would this ever really work? Could I actually make Be Au Sm my full-time career?

EMPOWERED BY BELIEF

That's when Chris Mills introduced me to Mike Holland, my CPA. Mike wasn't just a numbers guy—he was a visionary and someone who believed in empowering his clients. When we first met, I handed over my financials, and he started asking questions.

"What are your goals for Be Au Sm?" he asked. "Where do you see this going in the next year, three years, five years?"

I hesitated before answering. "Well, if I can finish my book, I'll be able to charge more for my keynotes . . . and if I can book fifty keynotes next year—"

Mike interrupted me. "You mean when."

"What?" I asked, caught off guard.

"You mean when you finish the book and when you book fifty keynotes," he said. "You keep saying 'if' you do this or that. You're too committed and focused on this to fail. It might not happen overnight, but it will happen."

His words stopped me in my tracks. To have someone like Mike believe in me like that was incredibly empowering. It was a pivotal moment for Be Au Sm. His confidence in my potential wasn't just encouraging—it was transformative. Most importantly, I believed him.

WORDS MATTER

Mike's belief in me gave me the push I needed to keep moving forward. Empowerment is about more than offering encouragement; it's about instilling confidence and shifting perspectives. Mike didn't just see the numbers in my financials; he saw the potential in my business and, more importantly, in me.

Empowerment comes from believing in others when they doubt themselves. It is our duty to remind them of what they're capable of and show them the path forward. That's what Mike did for me, and it changed everything.

Who in your life could use a lift right now? Words,—especially encouraging ones—are more powerful than we realize. A few thoughtful, empowering words could make all the difference in someone's life—just like Mike's words did for me.

42

YOUR CIRCLE OF FIVE

EMPOWERMENT

"We are the average of the five people we spend the most time with."

THIS QUOTE, OFTEN ATTRIBUTED to Jim Rohn, is more than just a catchy phrase—it's a life philosophy I not only believe but live by. Once I truly understood its meaning, I began to reexamine my inner circle. The people you spend your time with shape your thoughts, actions, and ultimately, your future. My personal and professional success—my happiness, even—is tied to the people I've chosen to surround myself with.

Remember that subtraction is just as important as addition. Sometimes, the biggest change you can make is removing negative influences from your life. One or two people constantly doubting your dreams or spewing negativity can derail even your best efforts. While your family—your spouse, children, and parents—shapes a huge part of who you are, the five closest friends or mentors you choose outside of your family often define your trajectory.

I'm fortunate to have more than five people in my circle who embody the values I hold dear and help me live my legacy every day. You've already met some of them—Ed Roshitsh, Mark Resnick, Paul Anastasi, and Les Trachtman. Now, let me tell you about three others: Scott Carpenter, Kenny Wertz, and Chris Mills.

SCOTT CARPENTER: THE SUPPORTER

Scott entered my life in 1997 when I was twenty-two and starting my first "real" job at ACT Software. He was my boss, but from the very beginning, he felt more like a friend.

I'll never forget our first company trip together to San Antonio, Texas. Scott and three other leaders invited me to dinner at Morton's Steakhouse. I'd never been to a high-end steakhouse before, and it was a night to remember—until the bill came.

"Why don't you take care of this one, Josh?" they said, poker-faced.

I laughed nervously, hoping they were kidding. "Just put it on your per diem," they said. I thought I was living the high life until I learned the next day that the per diem was $24—a fraction of what that fancy dinner cost. They got me good. To this day, Scott always pays the bill at Morton's because I never let him forget that story.

Scott has been much more than a dinner companion, though. He's been a mentor, a friend, and one of my biggest supporters. He's the one who drove me to my interview with SD in 2004, and when I left that company, he was one of the first to back my ventures with Be Au Sm.

Scott's leadership philosophy shaped how I approach teams and relationships. His mantra, "Inspire, not require," is something I live by. Effective leadership doesn't come from barking orders or micromanaging; it comes when you empower people to feel valued, motivated, and capable.

Scott has always given me the freedom to grow, and for that, I'm forever grateful.

KENNY WERTZ: THE SERVANT LEADER

Kenny wasn't my friend right away. As the facilities manager for Sharon Public Schools, Kenny had an impeccable reputation—funny, hardworking, and generous. He was someone I admired and wanted as a customer. I remember chasing him around a conference in 2004, trying to find my "in." By the next year, he became a client, and that marked the start of a lifelong friendship.

Kenny is the epitome of a servant leader. Every week, he and his family make sandwiches and deliver them to shelters. He's a quiet donor to countless charitable causes, never seeking recognition. He's also one of the most thoughtful people I know, always showing up with gourmet donuts or lending a listening ear when I need it most.

He's been by my side for some of my biggest challenges—literally. During both of my pumpkin river paddles, Kenny rowed alongside me for hours, encouraging me to keep going. Over the past eight years, not a single day has passed without us talking.

If you don't have a Kenny in your life, don't worry—they're rare. I count myself incredibly lucky to have him in mine.

CHRIS MILLS: THE COMMUNITY BUILDER

Chris Mills is a few years older than I am, but we've known each other since high school. We reconnected in 2018 at a volunteer fundraiser, and since then, he's been one of my closest friends.

Chris owns Chris Mills Construction and Shovel Town Flag Company, but he's much more than a business owner. He's a firefighter, paramedic, Board of Health member, and an active contributor to the Easton YMCA and the Silver Dollar Club. His heart for the community is unmatched.

Four years ago, an anonymous donor purchased a flag from Chris's company to honor veterans. The following year, Chris decided to take it further. Every day in November, he built and donated a flag to a veteran—thirty flags in thirty days. He's kept up the tradition ever since, paying for everything out of his own pocket.

Chris's actions remind me of the power of consistency—day after day, year after year, he shows up for his community, leading by example and inspiring others to do the same.

CURATING YOUR CIRCLE

The people you surround yourself with have an extraordinary impact on your life. They shape your thoughts, your mindset, and your ability to live your legacy. But building the right circle isn't just about finding people who inspire you—it's about having the courage to remove those who don't.

It's not an easy truth to accept, but not everyone in your life will have your best interests at heart. Some relationships, even long-standing ones, can become toxic or draining. Recognizing this and taking action is one of the hardest but most necessary steps toward growth. It's never easy to let go, but holding onto negativity or people who don't support your dreams only drags you down.

You can't just surround yourself with cheerleaders—being empowered requires curating a circle of people who challenge you, push you to be better, and remind you of your worth on the days you doubt it most. These are the people who show up consistently, who believe in you even when you struggle to believe in yourself.

Take a moment to reflect on your own circle: Who truly has your back? Who energizes you and helps you move forward? And who might be holding you back, intentionally or not? The answers to these questions are your guide to building a life of purpose, passion, and fulfillment.

Living your legacy begins with the people you choose to let into your life. The right circle doesn't just happen—it's built with intention, effort, and the occasional difficult conversation. But when you find your people, and you empower them as they empower you, that's when extraordinary things happen.

Remember, your legacy isn't just about what you do. It's about the connections you make, the lives you touch, and the people who will carry your impact forward long after you're gone. Choose your circle wisely.

And most importantly, choose to be the kind of person who belongs in someone else's circle too.

43

CONCLUSION

NOT LONG BEFORE WE finished writing this book, I picked up my youngest son, Chance, from school. He handed me a folded-up piece of paper and said, "Can you take this? I need to finish it when we get home."

Curious, I looked at his teacher, who smiled and said he was working on a fortune cookie. I unfolded the paper to find three words written in his handwriting: "When You Think."

I asked him what the rest was going to say, and he handed me another piece of paper that had been typed out: "When You Think Positive Thoughts, Good Things Happen!"

I couldn't help but smile. Chance has a way of capturing life's most profound truths with simple clarity.

Chance is our miracle. For a child we were told we'd never have, his wisdom is a daily reminder of the power of believing in good. I think he might have a future in writing fortune cookies—or perhaps inspiring others.

LIVING YOUR LEGACY WITH G.R.A.C.E.

Legacy isn't something you leave behind; it's something you live every day. That's the biggest realization I've had on this journey. For years, I thought of legacy as something tied to a name on a building or an achievement written in history books. But I've come to understand that legacy is much simpler—and much more powerful.

Your legacy is built in the moments you show up for others, the words you speak, the lessons you pass down, and the impact you make in the smallest, everyday ways. It's the life you live, not the one you leave.

When I launched Be Au Sm, I didn't have it all figured out. I wasn't chasing perfection, and I certainly wasn't trying to become an author, a speaker, or the face of a movement. I was simply trying to live better, to stop focusing on what I couldn't control and start living with intention. That intention became the foundation of G.R.A.C.E.

THE FRAMEWORK FOR LIVING YOUR LEGACY

I didn't just create these five elements—Gratitude, Resilience, Action, Consistency, and Empowerment—to fill the pages of a book or make a catchy acronym. I built them from real life. From personal struggles, heartbreaks, failures, and hard-earned lessons.

I've lived these principles, not because I always had it figured out but because life forced me to learn. I've been knocked down. I've doubted myself. I've waited too long to take action. But every time I chose to lean into these elements, my life changed for the better.

So, trust me when I say these five elements aren't abstract concepts. They are the playbook for living a meaningful, fulfilling life. They are tangible, actionable, and meant to be lived daily. And the best part? You don't need to master all of them at once. You just need to start. Small, intentional steps lead to profound change.

LEGACY BEGINS NOW

Don't keep waiting for the right time to live your legacy. Don't worry about hitting milestones, landing a promotion, or achieving something massive before you start making an impact. Concentrate on what you do today.

Every time you express gratitude, you are living your legacy.

Every time you resiliently push through adversity, you are living your legacy.

Every time you take action, you are living your legacy.

Every time you show up consistently, you are living your legacy.

Every time you empower someone else, you are living your legacy.

The truth is you're already creating your legacy, whether you realize it or not. The question is—are you living it the way you want to be remembered?

THE FINAL CHALLENGE

If you've made it this far, you're ready—ready to stop thinking of legacy as a destination instead of what it is: a daily decision.

My challenge to you is simple. Pick one element of G.R.A.C.E. and commit to it. If gratitude speaks to you, begin by sending one unexpected thank-you note this week. If resilience is what you need, choose one setback and decide to face it head-on. If action is calling your name, stop planning and start doing. If consistency is your struggle, commit to one small habit every day for the next month. And if empowerment is where you want to grow, reach out and lift someone up today.

The impact you make won't always be loud or obvious. Sometimes, it will be as simple as a kind word, a steady presence, or a lesson you pass on that someone carries for a lifetime. But make no mistake—that is how legacies are built. That is how they are lived.

You don't have to wait to be remembered. You just have to start living in a way worth remembering. Live with gratitude. Stand tall in resilience. Take bold action. Show up with consistency. And empower yourself and others every single day.

Take the first step, even if you're unsure where it will lead. Stop waiting for "someday" and start now because now is all we ever really have.

Thank you for being part of my journey, and remember, **if you can be anything—Be Au Sm.**

-Josh Peach

ACKNOWLEDGEMENTS

This book has been ten years in the making, and if there's one thing I've learned along the way, it's that nothing great is ever accomplished alone.

First, I want to thank Mark Resnick and his incredible team at Bellarmine Publishing. Mark, your belief in this book and your relentless dedication to getting it across the finish line has been nothing short of inspiring. Your expertise, guidance, and friendship have meant the world to me. I couldn't have done this without you.

To my family—thank you for your patience, your support, and your unwavering belief in me. You've allowed me the space to chase this dream, even when it meant late nights, early mornings, and way too many meetings at Target and Panera to work on this book.

To my mom, Ana, my dad, Eric, and Lola and Grandpa Pedro—for your love, support, and incredible sacrifices.

To my friends and colleagues who have walked alongside me on this journey—thank you for your encouragement, your honesty, and for always reminding me why this work matters. Your stories, challenges, and triumphs have shaped the very heart of this book.

To my *Be Au Sm* book sponsors—thank you for believing in the book's mission and for sharing its lessons with others. Whether you're gifting it to friends, colleagues, or a community group, your support helps spread the essential elements of G.R.A.C.E. far and wide. Your generosity and commitment to making a positive impact inspire me every day.

To everyone who has ever shared a moment of kindness, resilience, action, consistency, or empowerment—you are the reason Be Au Sm exists. You've inspired me in ways you may never realize, and I hope this book gives back even a fraction of what you've given me.

Finally, to you, the reader—thank you for showing up, for believing in something bigger, and for committing to living your legacy every single day. My greatest hope is that this book becomes a part of your journey, just as writing it has been a part of mine.

With gratitude,

-Josh

ABOUT THE AUTHORS

Joshua Peach is a renowned keynote speaker, entrepreneur, podcaster, and software executive. As the Founder of Be Au Sm, Josh has spent over a decade inspiring people to be their best in work and life, delivering more than 1,000 high-impact presentations across North America. His authentic storytelling and deep industry expertise make him a trusted voice on leadership, customer service, and personal growth. Josh lives in Easton, MA, with his fiance Amy and their two sons. To book Josh for your next keynote, visit **www.beausm.com.**

Mark J. Resnick is an award-winning author, a sought-after speaker, and a second-generation expert in branded merchandise. His impactful books, Ten Days With Dad 2)0))3 and The Greatest Burden The Greatest Blessing (2023), offer insights into resilience, caregiving, and the power of living with purpose. Through his writing, speaking engagements, and mentoring, Mark empowers individuals to redefine success and cultivate deeper fulfillment in their personal and professional lives. He resides in Walpole, MA, with his wife and three children. To book Mark, visit **www.markjresnick.com.**

LEGACY SPONSORS

Be Au Sm LEGACY sponsors provide invaluable momentum, confidence in our mission, and a genuine commitment to sharing the essential elements of G.R.A.C.E. far and wide. For this, we are truly grateful for your Au Sm support.

ESSENTIAL SPONSORS

Be Au Sm ESSENTIAL sponsors strengthen the foundation of our mission, ensuring that the principles of G.R.A.C.E. reach those who need them most. Your belief in this message fuels meaningful change, and we are deeply grateful.

GOLD SPONSORS

Be Au Sm Gold sponsors play a vital role in spreading the impact of G.R.A.C.E., supporting our journey with generosity and heart. Your commitment makes a difference, and we truly appreciate you.

Fred Makonnen

LEAVE A REVIEW

If *Be Au Sm: The Essential Elements to Living Your Life with G.R.A.C.E.* has inspired you, we'd love to hear from you! Taking just a few minutes to leave a review on Amazon or Goodreads helps others discover the book and spreads the message of living your legacy with G.R.A.C.E. worldwide.

Your review—whether a quick rating or a thoughtful reflection—can make a meaningful impact. Every shared experience helps more people embrace Gratitude, Resilience, Action, Consistency, and Empowerment in their own lives.

Leave an Amazon review in five easy steps.

- Go to Amazon and search for *Be Au Sm: The Essential Elements to Living Your Legacy with G.R.A.C.E.*
- Click on the Paperback or eBook version of our book.
- Below the Title and author names, you will see the 5.0 stars and to the right, the number of "ratings". Click on the ratings text (in the example below, it shows 155 ratings in blue; click that).
- The next screen is the review page. On the left-hand side, below Review this Product, click on the box that shows Write a Customer Review
- Click on the number of Stars (five is always nice), write your review, then hit submit at bottom right.

Ten Days With Dad: Finding Purpose, Passion, &
Peace During the Darkest Days of Alzheimer's and
COVID-19 Paperback – March 7, 2022
by Mark J. Resnick (Author), Bob Halloran (Foreword)

4.9 ★★★★★ ∨   155 ratings   See all formats and editions

Customer reviews
★★★★★ 4.9 out of 5
155 global ratings

5 star		91%
4 star		5%
3 star		4%
2 star		0%
1 star		0%

How customer reviews and ratings work ∨

★★★★★ Clear

Write a review
What should other customers know?

📷 Share a video or photo

Review this product

Share your thoughts with other customers

Write a customer review

Title your review (required)
What's most important to know?

Submit

Thank You!